DELIBERATIVE DEMOCRACY IN AMERICA

DELIBERATIVE DEMOCRACY IN AMERICA
A PROPOSAL FOR A POPULAR BRANCH OF GOVERNMENT

ETHAN J. LEIB

THE PENNSYLVANIA STATE UNIVERSITY PRESS
UNIVERSITY PARK, PENNSYLVANIA

Library of Congress Cataloging-in-Publication Data

Leib, Ethan J.
    Deliberative democracy in America : a proposal for a popular
    branch of government / Ethan J. Leib.
        p.   cm.
    Includes bibliographical references and index.
    ISBN 0-271-02363-5 (cloth : alk. paper)
    1. Direct democracy—United States. 2. Representative government
    and representation—United States. 3. Civil society—United States.
    4. Legitimacy of governments—United States. 5. Social choice—
    United States. I. Title.

JF494.L45 2004
320.973'01—dc22   2003015486

The Pennsylvania State University Press is a member of the Association
of American University Presses.

It is the policy of The Pennsylvania State University Press to use acid-free
paper. Publications on uncoated stock satisfy the minimum requirements
of American National Standard for Information Sciences—Permanence of
Paper for Printed Library Material, ANSI Z39.48–1992.

Every page of *The Federalist Papers* is a call to the people of America to take its fate into its own hands and to fashion its institutions in the light of the best political science of the present rather than to look timidly to the past. The good citizen of today can do no less.

—*Judith Shklar* (1990, 10)

The truth is that no part of the present-day government is well suited, by virtue of practical capacity or political intervention, to undertake the job of structural and episodic reconstruction [of the political public sphere]. The mission lacks—as every novel and serious mission in the world does—its proper agent. The best response, then, is to forge the new agent: *another branch of government,* another power in the state, designed, elected, and funded with the express charge of carrying out this distinctive rights-ensuring work. Such a move, however, would demand the very openness to institutional experimentalism in which contemporary law and contemporary democracies have proved so remarkably deficient.

—*Roberto Mangabeira Unger* (1996, 32–33) (*emphasis added*)

CONTENTS

I always read acknowledgments first. Not only because they usually begin books—even when they are at the end, I cannot bear the suspense—but also because I tend to judge people by those intimates and colleagues with whom they surround themselves. Moreover, too often in academic writing, authors hide themselves everywhere else, and acknowledgments can be a brief window into the humanity behind the labor and production of scholarship. Finally, I was influenced early by Martin Heidegger's (1968, 138–47) insight that the German *Denken* and *Danken,* the Old English *thencan* and *thancian,* and the English *to think* and *to thank* are perhaps more than "assonance": he insists in *What is Called Thinking?* that there is a deep connection between thinking and thanking, that thought "implies the thanks" (139). Even if his etymology can be criticized (see, e.g., Bourdieu 1991, 75), Heidegger got me thinking that I could not think without thanking: all citations to other authors are expressions of gratitude; all scholarship is simultaneous thinking and thanking.

Sometimes acknowledgments testify to someone's goodness and they can't help but be charming. Consider James C. Scott (1976, ix): "I wish . . . to report that my wife and children, who have their own scholarly and other concerns, had virtually nothing to do with this volume. They were not particularly understanding or helpful when it came to research and writing but called me away as often as possible to the many pleasures of a life in common. May it always remain so." Sometimes acknowledgments testify to someone's potential strangeness. Consider Leslie Brisman's (1990, 121) ode: "And to Harold Bloom, Genius of the Shore: I acknowledge all the good of thy large influence, however accompanied by sad dismay at my wandering in too normative a flood." Or consider Will Kymlicka's (1995, vi) final thanks: "I would like to thank Codie and Luke. Like most dogs, they are baffled, and sometimes exasperated, by the amount of time humans spend poring over the printed word. But they kept me company on some long nights, and I am grateful for that."

Romantic life, generally a reliable source for heartfelt acknowledgment, is not as dependable for young authors like myself. During the publication process of my first article, for example, I needed to call the printer's office at the last minute to have a partner's name removed: even after three years together, the ex wanted no association in print. There are complexities to the thank-you when romantic life is in transition: Does one thank the partner who was the companion during the writing even if a new relationship supports the submission process? What if there is a very promising relationship that may continue in perpetuity, but started only when the page proofs came in? If a book is forever along with the gratitude inside it, wouldn't the author want to acknowledge the new love as a testimony to its promise? Should one be promiscuous and thank all previous lovers no matter the effect on one's current partner? These are hard questions that I won't attempt to answer. Someone has already written a book about marginalia (Jackson 2001) and a book about the footnote (Grafton 1999); it is time for someone to do a study of acknowledgments. I suppose Gertrude Stein (1994) wrote *A Novel of Thank You,* but, as she tells us, that novel is a novel "of thank you and not about it" (185).

Unfortunately, going to law school and being forced to read the law reviews has somewhat soured my taste for acknowledgments. In law reviews, as often in the law, instrumental rationality prevails: even gratitude is professionalized as authors, eager to convince law students to accept their pieces for publication, produce a formidable and often disingenuous list of acknowledgments to suggest that each enumerated name actually read and endorsed the manuscript under consideration. I have no intention of gaining credibility by association: the people I thank here actually helped to make this book possible. The usual disclaimer applies, though: all errors are my parents' fault.

I wish to thank Yale and my parents for financial support; John Delury, Aaron Matz, and David Ponet for moral support; Bruce Ackerman, Seyla Benhabib, Cynthia Farrar, Abe Goldstein, Ian Shapiro, and Rogers Smith for intellectual support; David Grosz for editorial support; and Sandy Thatcher for publication support. Thanks also to Archon Fung and Kevin Mattson who read the entire manuscript and provided important criticisms and insights, dramatically improving the finished product. Finally, portions of this book have been published previously in the *Rutgers Law Journal,* and I thank the editors of that journal for the permission to reprint those portions here.

Ethan J. Leib, New Haven, Conn.

INTRODUCTION

There is a lot of talk in political theory these days. And among the most talked about topics is talking itself: theories of deliberative democracy are colonizing the entire discipline. Hundreds of books have been written to map the territory staked out by the various theories, each making an effort to find an uninhabited little island where some new theoretical development can get under way. The central principle of deliberative democracy can be summarized as follows: "At the heart of the deliberative conception of democracy is the view that collective decision-making is to proceed deliberatively—by citizens advancing proposals and defending them with considerations that others, who are themselves free and equal, can acknowledge as reasons" (Cohen and Sabel 1997, 327).

However, what started as a theoretical enterprise to justify certain kinds of reasons and decision-making processes has now also captured the attention of institutional designers. Democrats who appreciate the value of deliberation in democratic decision-making routinely conjure technocratic tools to invigorate deliberation in democracy under the theoretically well established view that deliberation contributes to legitimacy. Since Jürgen Habermas (1996) promulgated the view that communicative power coming from the subjects of a regime may be one of the only sources for the legitimation of state power, communication and deliberation have become the focus of democrats interested in finding ways for the voice of the people to be heard more loudly, providing a forum for the rulers to heed the informed views of the ruled. Accordingly, this book exercises institutional imagination; it offers a reform proposal to begin the conversation about how we can better design our political institutions to conform to the aspirations of deliberative democracy, since the literature has been much more voluminous in theory than in practice. But let us take one step back before moving forward.

WHAT IS THE ILL FOR WHICH DELIBERATION IS THE CURE?

While deliberation is the medicine many theorists and some general practitioners are willing to prescribe, the diagnosis of the current regime's sickness is sometimes elusive. And if we don't know the disease and its etiology, the cure and its own side effects and pathologies are really secondary. Lucky for us, the problem is usually rather inviting to deliberative democrats: our democracy is not deliberative enough. But we must say a bit more.

There are a number of basic problems with our version of republican democracy that come to mind rather easily if we keep an ideal of popular sovereignty in view. Generally, voters select among candidates with a bundle of policy commitments that cannot be disentangled; federal lawmaking in accordance with Article I, section 7, of the United States Constitution leaves most bills losing steam prior to passage; the committee system is vulnerable to manipulation; divided government often renders legislatures impotent; and the policies that are enacted are often selected by lawmakers for less than kosher reasons (pork-barreling, rent-seeking, log-rolling, etc.). When voters take matters into their own hands through the initiative or referendum, they act out of ignorance or self-interest (rational or not), under the influence of mass media campaigns that are often aimed to misinform; and poor turnouts cast a further shadow of suspicion over electoral results (especially when the poor and minorities are underrepresented or undercounted). Unfortunately, many democratic theorists are willing to accept these losses because they imagine that our democracy is pretty good anyway; indeed, even voters who suffer the failures of democracy accept this trade-off, simply because to them it isn't worth the effort to become more involved or informed. Or perhaps because they do not believe they could do any good. Yet it remains unclear how we can all stay sanguine about our version of democracy when its built-in limitations are so manifold and obvious. Participatory democrats—those who favor greater levels of political participation—tend to justify their preferences by noting that broadened participation may ameliorate some of the defects associated with mass democracy: citizens can pool information and ideas, bring local knowledge to the table, establish greater levels of equality and political opportunity, and the like. But it is important to remember that these democrats usually do not take the power inequalities to be the primary problem: instead they target for reform the process failures that foster and facilitate them.

To be sure, some efforts in structural reform have the aforementioned problems in view when they set their sights on a new vision for American democracy. Campaign finance reform proposals are, perhaps, the most salient examples of recent energies directed to alter the system of democracy as we know it. Many bright ideas have been proffered in service of the basic insight that if we get money out of politics, we can get a politics that is both more legitimate and less steered by the rich. The distortion of money can make democracy a joke; the masses can serve as the marionettes of money managers and make decisions that cannot help but help the capitalists, who are very good at convincing others that their fate is wholly tied to the strength of the economy and, in turn, the strength of the capitalists. We all know who pulls the strings.

Proposals for consultation regimes, where policymakers and bureaucrats confer with the electorate to tailor their rulemaking to the needs of their constituency, are another common palliative for the sorts of problems described earlier. Policy planners often prescribe that administrators speak directly with the people in a nonthreatening environment to heed their concerns and maybe even change policy accordingly. Of course, those consulted are often self-selected repeat players who are rarely heeded.

There are even those who espouse a completely different decision-procedure for our (by and large) two-party majoritarian voting system. Whether it is a proposal for proportional representation, cumulative voting, or the proliferation of parties, there is no dearth of suggestions that American democracy could be made stronger by revamping political life as we know it.

On a smaller scale, the call for more local and accountable government is yet another version of a cure for the ills of mass democracy. Proponents of local government worry that citizens do not have enough input into decision-making processes and have little control over how their interests are represented. They also imagine that community concerns are more likely to be considered if the community can govern more consistently with its own values.

Each of these proposed republican reforms of government (and of course a republican form of government is guaranteed by Article IV of the United States Constitution) has a diagnosis that allows us—in the felicitous phrase of Jon Elster (1998, 10)—to argue for arguing, to make an argument for why deliberation is well suited to the task of ameliorating the condition of mass democracy. The condition can be summed up by noting that our democracy suffers a *legitimacy deficit:* citizens are so remote from decision-making that the decisions rendered in their name cannot be fairly imputed to them and their authorship. If this is indeed the problem, deliberative democracy may, after all, be a viable solution that encourages institutional redesign from within the general framework we already have in place.

LET'S GET THE SHOW ON THE ROAD

This book starts by getting right down to the business of design. It proposes a fourth branch of government to make laws using randomly selected civic juries, wholly displacing the referendum and initiative systems as they exist today. I make my assumptions clear: where political autonomy is measured by the degree to which people can be said to be the authors of their own laws, deliberation by ordinary citizens helps the republican project of self-authorship. I also take for granted that face-to-face democracy has benefits that teledemocracy can never provide. I may be a Luddite, but I am fairly sure cyberspace isn't yet the place for democracy so long as there is a digital divide or a delay in perceiving the emotions a face can convey.

I argue that the system of checks and balances remains unbalanced and that representative government is not well suited to the task of popular sovereignty. The people need a voice of their own, but referendums have failed to provide a reliable one. A fourth branch—not the media or the administrative agencies—is needed to get the people to speak in topically specified ways that are not distorted by money, expertise, or naked power. Deliberation is a value because it is a response to the distortions, but neither the legislature nor the judiciary is sufficiently deliberative to be the trustee of deliberative democracy. So we need a deliberative branch—what I call the *popular* branch—to do this work. The first chapter makes this argument, while also giving a summary of how to operationalize it.

Here are some of the operations: There is a commission responsible for its administration, which has representatives from each of the parties as well as independents. There are ways for the legislatures, the judiciaries, and the people themselves to try to get a question onto the popular agenda. And while the design is intended for the national political arena, there are corollary possibilities for any state or city system.

There is compulsory service, required to get a proper representative sample deliberating; since each deliberative assembly of the branch could only accommodate 525 people, it is necessary to make sure the people are not subject to the voluntary response problem. I propose a decision procedure (a supermajority requirement) and an implementation stage, where the branch's activities get absorbed into the separation of powers. These details help ensure that the popular branch, when it utters its decision, is actually reflective of a popular *will*, not merely a public opinion.

Chapter 1 also offers more details for the design. It explains how participants are to be selected (random stratified sampling); how we can be assured of citizen competence (empirical work); how we can moderate the pathologies of deliberative environments (a design problem to be tackled with efforts in education and moderation); how we can design ground rules for what people are allowed to say (no gag rules); whom we can put in the room to make sure discussion is well informed and civil (federal judges or volunteers from the League of Women Voters); and who gets to be considered stakeholders (virtually everyone). Many of the details here are elaborations of James Fishkin's work with Deliberative Polling, and I make the connections between the popular branch and Deliberative Polling explicit (as well as exploring my deviations therefrom).

The second chapter is a theoretical one, explaining the model of deliberative democracy I use to support my proposal. It assumes certain legitimacy deficits in current republican democracy that deliberation is well suited to address. It takes the legitimacy problem developed from a respect for popular sovereignty as much more basic than the problems associated with power inequalities; it is more interested in procedures than in ensuring fundamental rights. The argument here leaves to other branches the protection against the tyranny of the majority. Instead, the focus here is upon garnering a majority informed and representative enough to heed in the first place.

Since much of the institutionalization of the popular branch, however, hinges on how the separation of powers would function in this possible polity, the third and fourth chapters are devoted to this issue. Participatory democrats rarely give any attention to how popular deliberation can be institutionalized; and when they institutionalize it, they invariably displace so many other governmental functions that the resulting regime is unrecognizable. Either they take the practices of deliberative democracy as they see them or propose unrealistic reforms. Deliberative assemblies cannot do everything, but they also cannot merely be in civil society without having a binding effect on the state: they need to be institutionalized as mechanisms of the state and be able to issue binding statements of popular will. Chapters 3 and 4 are poised to address the most difficult design question: how can a "popular" branch be integrated and coordinated with the representative presidentialist system we have now? The reform proposal offered here is not meant to be wholly revolutionary and displace all governmental units; nevertheless, it is meant to provide a forum for revolutionary politics where higher lawmaking is possible (even if most of the time the polity is satisfied with ordinary politics).

In Chapter 3 I start thinking through Arendt's objections to Jefferson's council system and the family resemblance of my proposal with his. I consider what my proposal might do to the two-party system. I make my way through similar ideas that the Progressives tried, offering the lack of attention to integration and the separation of powers as one reason for their failure.[1] By arguing that the failure to institutionalize deliberative assemblies was sure to lead to their irrelevance, I lay the groundwork for Chapter 4.

Chapter 4 offers the actual integration exercise. I take two policy proposals through the popular system, showing what the branch would look like in action. I discuss each traditional branch's relationship to and authority over the popular branch—and how the legislative, executive, or judiciary branches could try to mobilize it. Ultimately, after making my way through the legislature, the executive, and the judiciary, I tackle the question of judicial review of the work of the popular branch. Only then do I revisit the question of the party system and its potential integration into the branch's activities.

Chapters 5 and 6 are meant to deflect the suspicions that the first four chapters are sure to raise. They address such questions as: Why do I require a two-thirds "supermajority" to enact a law at the assemblies? Why isn't half enough? Are juries so reliable that we should depend upon them in the *legislative* process? What of the use of the jury analogy altogether? Isn't there empirical evidence that controverts Fishkin, showing incompetence and inefficiency in actual practices of deliberation? Don't these deliberative assemblies, in a sense, force people to be free? Isn't the use of coercion offensive to liberal republicans? Couldn't deliberative assemblies be corrupted, just like any easily targeted small group of decision-makers? Shouldn't citizens have access to the goings-on of all deliberative assemblies and understand how the members of the jury arrive at their decisions? Doesn't the "value of publicity" demand the transparency of the procedure? Wouldn't excessive secrecy shroud its legitimacy? While these questions seem rather specific, many of the details of the proposal—especially

---

1. To be sure, there are many others reasons for their failure. Archon Fung thinks the Red Scare was the most obvious reason. I try to offer in Chapter 3 a less obvious account.

details like compulsory service—require explicit rejoinders. Chapter 6, on the jury and compulsory service, is an original contribution because so many theorists in the public policy literature pay too little attention to the voluntary response problem associated with most consultation regimes. Even institutional designers sensitive to the value of deliberation underestimate the need to have a truly representative sample culled for deliberation—representing even those who often prefer not to speak or volunteer their time for civic affairs.

Finally, Chapter 7, the conclusion of the design project, explores what role civil society (that is, nongovernmental associations) may play in setting the agenda for the deliberative publics. It explores how nondeliberative bodies will have to compete for opportunities to have their issues heard by a deliberative body such as the popular branch, and makes an effort to show why civil society must and how civil society can take the agenda-setting function away from complete elite control.

After discussing some theoretical work on the role of civil society in a deliberative democracy, I offer a number of ways that citizens in civil society (those not selected for popular activities on a given subject) could gain practical access to the political public sphere (the popular branch). I offer a mild version of interest-group pluralism, where civil associations garner signatures to get issues before the branch. I suggest that civil associations might get themselves on Yea/Nay committees organized to help present arguments to the deliberators in plenary sessions. I recommend a version of Bruce Ackerman's (1993) "Patriot Proposal," where every citizen would get fifty points to allocate funds to the civil associations of his or her choice. Concurrently, civil associations would be trying to win citizen points in and for media campaigns to influence the Yea/Nay committees. If successful, the committees would include their arguments in the pamphlet of materials the deliberators ultimately receive. I also suggest that candidates may run on a platform of sending something to the popular branch (which they often do in states that make substantial use of the direct democracy procedures of the initiative and referendum), another way the general electorate could control the agenda of the popular branch.

The epilogue very briefly sketches how activists interested in establishing a popular branch might help facilitate its birth (and the rebirth of democracy). Obviously, a national constitutional amendment would probably be necessary for the version offered in the book to take effect. But the scope and jurisdiction of the proposal need not reform the entire country all at once: states and municipalities could first engage in a little "democratic experimentalism," in the phrase of Dorf and Sabel (1998), before the country adopted a national version of the proposal.

Let us proceed to the proposal itself. I hope to demonstrate that my popular branch would not only ameliorate legitimacy deficits, but also (if only obliquely) help mitigate the problems associated with money in politics, political alienation, political ignorance, legislative deadlock from the current separation of powers, and the pathologies of individualism in mass democracy. While I don't spend a lot of time explaining how the proposal forwards each of these advantages, I hope the reader will be able to keep these potentialities in view when considering the viability and desirability of the proposal.

1

GETTING RIGHT DOWN TO THE
BUSINESS OF DESIGN

Discussions about deliberative democracy are notoriously short on proposals for practical institutional reform. Joshua Cohen (1997, 85) may be right that we will need a lot more data from political psychologists before we can reasonably take a stab at proposing such reforms. But it is also imperative to engage in the "nuts and bolts" debate of just what kinds of changes we discourse theorists or deliberative democrats want to effect. Amy Gutmann and Dennis Thompson (1996, 1) claim that deliberative democracy is "in search of a theory." I think it is in search of an operationalized practice. I wish to give some serious consideration to Unger's (1996, 32–33) call for a new branch of government. He never provided any details; I hope not to provide too many.

Some theorists have not been so shy about putting forward practical ideas on behalf of institutionalized deliberation. Robert Dahl (1970, 149–50; 1989, 340) has suggested that each citizen be required to serve on an advisory council to an elected official for a single year. The advisory board's membership would be in constant electronic correspondence with one another and would serve as an institutional mechanism to check representatives at the legislative level. This is not substantially different from Peter deLeon's (1997) endorsement of what he terms Participatory Policy Analysis (PPA), where randomly selected citizens who might plausibly be affected by a particular policy are conscripted to meet expert policymakers and bureaucrats to give their input into administrative matters over the course of a year. Notoriously undemocratic, the administrative bodies that make critical governmental decisions might benefit from consultation and deliberation with some lay citizens. John Burnheim (1985, 111–13) has more radically called for the end of representative democracy as we know it. Instead, he would like to institutionalize deliberation by having small random samples of citizens debate various political issues and set policy for the polity as a whole. And James Fishkin (1991; 1997; 1999a; Fishkin and Robert Luskin 1999), less radically and with greater caution, has argued that public opinion polls should be replaced with (what he terms and trademarks) "Deliberative Polls," where approximately five hundred people gather to debate issues and come to more informed public opinions. The polls are designed to represent more accurately what an informed body would decide if it were equipped with relevant information to make a decision, precisely the kind of information voters often lack. By using random samples to make policy *recommendations,* Fishkin hopes to achieve deliberative input into governmental units while revitalizing civic participation more generally as citizens get themselves informed. But, in effect, he leaves all governmental institutions untouched by deliberation, or capable of ignoring popular will, because the deliberations are only involved in processes of opinion-formation.[1]

Here I would like to try to synthesize a reform proposal of my own based upon three major assumptions. Without argument, I assume a largely discourse-theoretic view of democracy that takes for granted the republican virtue of collective self-government as well as the Kantian claim that each citizen should be the author of his or her own laws. This democratic intuition has been aptly described as follows: "Popular political self-government is first of all the ongoing social project of authorship of a country's fundamental laws by the country's people in some nonfictively attributable sense" (Michelman 1997,

---

1. Fishkin's work—in conjunction with the work of Ned Crosby, who studies civic juries (a term he has trademarked)—has spawned a literature into which this book neatly fits. My proposal differs from the others offered in this literature—in ways that I will try not to belabor. In general, the ones with a "family resemblance" are by Benjamin Barber (1984); John Gastil (2000); Ned Crosby, Jane Kelly, and Paul Schaefer (1986); Ned Crosby (1995); and Simon Threlkeld (1998). I discuss Crosby and Gastil in more detail in Chapter 6. Though I developed my idea before finding Threlkeld's five-page comment, it turns out that the ideas there are remarkably similar to the ones here. My proposal, however, is far more developed and less utopian than his and, unlike his, respects the current regime of representation and separation of powers (something Barber's assuredly does not do either). Moreover, Threlkeld and Barber suffer an infinite regress problem because they want to see citizen juries do everything, even though they pay virtually no attention to the agenda-setting problem.

145–47). I further assume that our constitutional democracy attempts to approximate this virtue for its citizenry by aggregating preferences and sanctioning some rule by majority, all while checking people's preferences by enforcing some basic norms of equality.[2] The last major assumption I make is that face-to-face citizen interaction more closely embodies democratic ideals than representative bodies or virtual/electronic communication.[3]

I try to steer clear of clarifying the foundational defenses for fundamental rights that are inviolable by majorities—this is the task of much political theory and provides much of the justification for judicial review and the separation of powers.[4] Instead, I want to focus upon the dynamics of how better to approximate our approximation of democracy. I want to find a way to tweak our current system to make it more generally desirable (making the three assumptions with respect to what counts as desirable). I expect that the proposal should be attractive to democrats and republicans (lowercase "d" and "r") of all colors as long as they are not elitist liberals, who are generally distrustful that people *should* be the authors of their own laws. As long as "we the people" are not treated as a political fiction impossible to conceive or

2. For an elaborate explanation of the uses and disadvantages of majoritarianism for life, see Gutmann and Thompson 1996, 27–33. In this proposal, supermajorities play a role, which requires a somewhat different strategy of defense; see Chapter 5.

3. Iris Marion Young (1990) makes a good case for why face-to-face relations ought not necessarily be privileged. She claims that "the ideal [of face-to-face democracy] presumes a myth of unmediated social relations, and wrongly identifies mediation with alienation. . . . It implies a model of the good society as consisting of decentralized small units which is both unrealistic and politically undesirable, and which avoids the political question of just relations among such decentralized communities" (232–33). She considers such a model "wildly utopian" and thinks "a model of a transformed society must begin from the material structures that are given to us at this time in history" (233–34). Last, she urges that "politics must be conceived as a relationship of strangers who do not understand one another in a subjective and immediate sense, relating across time and distance" (234). As will become evident here, I actually agree with (and account for) many of Young's perspectives and think my proposal addresses some of her concerns by keeping room for less "direct-democratic" and more representative institutions, while ultimately endorsing a face-to-face deliberative model.

I am most convinced of the virtues of face-to-face democracy when considering what Elaine Scarry (1996, 98) has called "the difficulty of imagining other people." By insisting on the opacity of the other, Scarry's argument takes account of Young's critiques of liberalism. Of course, Scarry recruits this "difficulty" to establish a justification for constitutionalism over cosmopolitan largesse, whereas I see deliberative democracy as a potential source for helping us with this difficulty—the difficulty that we cannot act on behalf of others unless we know or confront them in some non-fictive sense. In his more romantic moments, Fishkin seems to justify deliberative democracy along similar lines, especially when telling us anecdotes of radical paradigm shifts in people's attitudes when they come to appreciate the situation of an other in the course of his polling weekends.

4. For a proposal on how better to ensure democratic values through the separation of powers, see Bruce Ackerman's defense of "constrained parliamentarianism" in Ackerman 2000.

construct in reality, my proposal looks to give substance to what the rhetorical refrain or reification could mean, in the best of cases. Even if William Riker (1982) is right that Americans are governed by institutions, and not themselves, American institutions can use more direct input from institutionalized deliberation, ensuring better levels of self-government. And the critics of deliberative democracy who see it as "rule by the articulate" (Epstein 1988, 1642),[5] or as insensitive to power relations (Shapiro 1999b; Young 1990, 233–34),[6] should see in my proposal mechanisms to allay their concerns, helping them trust the people, whom they claim to want to help.

THE PROPOSAL

I propose adding a new branch of government to our system of checks and balances. In addition to the executive, legislative, and judicial branches, the people need to have a more distinct voice in a branch of their own. Let us call such a branch *popular* insofar as it aims to instantiate our ideas about popular sovereignty more concretely. As a practical matter, this branch would replace the initiative and the referendum; its institution would be established to address many of the shortcomings of those forms of direct democracy. Its functions could be brought about through national or state constitutional amendments,[7] and its findings would enact laws—laws that could be repealed or vetoed by the relevant (state or federal) executive or legislative branch (with a supermajority), or could be challenged in the judicial branch. Though these vehicles for overruling popular decisions should be available in any conception of the institutional design, I would suspect that they would not often be exercised for fear of evidencing a patina of contravening political mandates.

Composed of stratified random samples of 525 eligible—though not necessarily registered—voters, debating in groups of approximately fifteen, the popular branch would take the form of small civic juries occasionally meeting

5. More recently, some have lashed out against "pluralistic logocracy" (Cohen and Sabel 1997, 330). But as Cohen and Sabel astutely note, "The potential for deliberative failure is no argument against efforts at [deliberative] improvement."

6. For a comprehensive argument that one should be suspicious of my entire enterprise, see Sanders 1997. Sanders's argument is well worth attending to, though my project addresses many of her concerns with deliberative institutions.

7. Ironically, I need to depend on the functions of the other branches to "create" my newly devised check on their authority. Of course, I never deny the legitimacy of nondeliberative governmental actions altogether, so this feature should become less ironic as the discussion proceeds.

in plenary sessions to get their "charges." Such juries would debate political policies at assemblies convened for such purposes and would be modeled on Fishkin's Deliberative Polls, administered with the degree of care that Fishkin takes to make his Deliberative Polls representative, unbiased, and informed. Such juries would be called in circumstances where ballot initiatives and referendums are currently employed in the states that use them. In this paradigm, the popular branch would have the authority to enact law, while the legislative and executive branches would help with setting the agendas and tailoring the findings of the deliberative body into coherent written statutes. They would also be responsible, as they are now, for dealing with law-making processes so specialized as to have no substantial popular interest.

Jurisdiction of the popular branch would depend on the policy question at issue; both local and federal questions could be settled by representative samples of citizens, though each would have slightly different but analogous procedures to bring about the "deliberative" settling of questions.[8] In the case of national assemblies, it would probably be better to have several regional conventions where vote totals are aggregated, not weighted—one person, one vote. Even large states might require regional samples for their state-wide popular activities.

Political concerns about which every citizen can have an informed opinion (for example, gay marriage, drug legislation, or presumed consent for organ donation) would be put to a group of random citizens to decide over the course of a few days either at the state or national level. Often these types of political opinions are remarkably uninformed; and since these are the issues likely to find themselves on the agenda, the deliberative assembly would help settle questions that demand more thoughtful consideration by the electorate.

I would impose a relatively high threshold for putting the question to a policy jury from the direct democratic route of agenda-setting (what could now be known as the *popular* initiative process). Thus, ten percent of the relevant voting population would need to agree to place a proposal on the deliberative agenda (not agree to the proposal itself), and the signatures of those advocates would need to be geographically distributed throughout the state or nation in

---

8. I do not mean to suggest that deliberative juries could not be used for many other purposes at the administrative level. I view my proposal as consistent with, though not dependent upon, such efforts. Most specifically, I am interested in seeing how Fishkin's creation can be utilized to establish a better political public sphere, where decisions are a product of deliberative will-formation.

some equitable fashion.[9] Given the proliferation of e-correspondence, e-mail signatures could count for the direct popular mechanism, but ways to curb corruption, a common problem with signature-gathering in general, would be needed. Perhaps Colorado's current practice is exemplary: a random sample of the signatures representative of the whole list is drawn and only the selected names get verified (Magleby 1995, 22–23).

From the less direct democratic route, the referendum, a supermajority of one legislative house along with a simple majority of the other—another high threshold—could send an item onto the popular agenda for adjudication. Because legislators are already trained in the ways of statute-drafting, it would be advantageous to have joint committees draft statutes for popular consideration. Since the drafters would know that their bills would ultimately be subject to the careful scrutiny of the jurors of the popular branch, they would be forced to be clear and specific if they want to achieve popular acceptance. Riders would fall by the wayside.

After achieving acceptance from the popular branch, a law would need to be signed by the president (or governor). To be sure, the executive and legislative branches (with an appropriate supermajority) could veto the popular branch's decision, assuming they were willing to risk impeachment or recall for contravening the informed will of the people.

Finally, judges at the appellate level (in both the federal and state court systems) could, by a mere *en banc* majority, convene a popular assembly to settle a popular question. Of course, in the case of convocation by the judiciary, the popular branch would have more of a recommending and informational capacity than a lawmaking one. The branch's decisions would not be binding only because in this kind of affair, more similar to the Fishkin model, citizens would not be debating law, but public opinion. In this manner, both representative and direct mechanisms could place an item on the popular agenda and have input into all branches of government.

Such a new branch of government would require a new body of administration in charge of regulating, organizing, and preparing the deliberative jury process. Such an agency would process requests for adjudication by deliberative assembly, which could come from the legislatures, the judiciaries, or the people themselves. The administrative body would make sure the early stages of statute-drafting and signature-garnering proceeded without corruption by

9. In 1992, of the twenty-seven states that had some form of initiative or referendum, one-third of them had a signature threshold at ten percent or above. Of those nine, seven were at ten percent, so I arbitrarily follow those states (Magleby 1995, 22). The geographic distribution criterion could be flexible depending on what locale is most affected by the policy at issue.

moneyed interests. During the preparation of the informational and factual materials to be used as the bases for deliberation, the administrative body would help pare down and focus the debate, making it "debatable" over the course of three or four days. But their contribution would be procedural, not substantive, assuming that such a distinction is tenable. As an example of what such a body might look like, consider Arne Leonard's (1995, 1236) vision of a statewide "Citizen's Commission on Constitutional Amendment" (CCCA):

> An independent commission to consist of nine members . . . which shall be composed of six appointed members and three elected members. Each of the following state officials shall appoint one person to serve as a member of the CCCA: the Speaker of the House of Representatives; the President Pro Tempore of the Senate; the Governor; the Attorney General; the Chief Justice of the Supreme Court; and the Chief Judge of the Court of Appeals. No more than three of the appointed members of the CCCA shall be from the same political party. Registered electors shall elect three members of the CCCA [directly]. Elected members of the CCCA may not simultaneously hold another elected state office. All members of the CCCA shall serve for a term of four years from the date they are elected or appointed . . . [and] shall prescribe its own rules of order and procedure in accordance with the State Administrative Procedure Act. The legislature shall provide suitable quarters for the CCCA, appropriate funds for its lawful expenses, and compensate its members for their services.

Mutatis mutandis, this kind of commission could be replicated at different levels of government (municipal, state, and federal) and could help administer deliberative assemblies and arbitrate among stakeholders, as well as maintain the integrity of the deliberative process. Leonard wants to institutionalize this commission to help make initiatives and referendums more deliberative; my proposal goes further to counteract the dynamics of mass democracy evidenced in the general initiative and referendum procedures currently in place. Because I do not rely strictly on the educative potential of deliberation, and because I care about its potential for popular will–formation, I require a much deeper reorganization of initiatives and referendums.

In my adaptation of Leonard's council, I would continue to allow parties to play some role and thus leave seats on the relevant commission for party appointments. The parties would be able to appoint members to the popular branch, but no more than three appointees (of the nine sitting members at each level) could be from the same party. I expect that there would be state commissions for state and local questions and a national commission for federal questions, so the business of who gets to make the appointments would depend on the particular jurisdiction of the administrative body. Leonard's proposal is for a statewide body, but, realistically, the general party structure would run the confirmation proceedings, regardless of what level of government the council oversees. Let the parties do the work of appeasing each other and the public.

But the last three members (the swing votes) would be elected directly by voters. The candidates for these offices would not be able to take money from any party for their campaigns. Instead, the citizens running for popular office (notice here that an administrative agency would have elected commissioners) could only apply for public money to help run their campaigns after jumping through the usual hoops that candidates always must. Their campaigns could only be funded with public monies or personal fortunes, and no private interests would be allowed to use their weight for even independent expenditures. Maybe this would mean that only people like Jon Corzine, Steve Forbes, and Ross Perot could afford to run. But their role is mostly to shuffle through papers and proposals and summarize contents, work that their staffs would do with greater precision in any event. To be sure, my assumption that the agencies would be value-free is optimistic at best. But with procedural measures to ensure the integrity of the branch and with the publicity associated with every step of the process, the scrutiny of the mass media and the general population could probably keep the administrative body in check.

One of the greatest problems with current initiative and referendum procedures is that, by and large, only groups with substantial financial backing can afford to garner the necessary signatures to get a proposal on the ballot or fund the media campaigns often necessary to force a legislative referendum (Magleby 1995, 36). Even in my model, special interest groups with a lot of cash will be more likely to be able to get their initiatives considered by a deliberative body. But one of the main purposes for my proposal is to take away some of the power of the purse by subjecting each proposed policy to deliberative bodies, not to an uninformed, unrepresentative minority of voters very susceptible to manipulation by efforts taken in the mass media. Mass democracy suffers from this problem, brought about by an undisciplined populism (Magleby 1995, 37–40). Consider this evidence:

> Most voters face an informational vacuum. . . . Previous research has
> demonstrated that significant numbers vote in ways inconsistent with

their preferences on the issue generally. Take the case of a 1980 California rent control initiative. . . . Citing its exit poll, the *Los Angeles Times* concluded that "voters apparently ended up confused and suspicious of the proposition." Analysis of this exit poll demonstrates that more than half of all California voters were confused about what a "yes" and "no" vote meant. Over three-fourths of California voters did not match their views on rent control with their vote on the proposition: twenty-three percent wanted to protect rent control but incorrectly voted "yes," and fifty-four percent were opposed to rent control but incorrectly voted "no." (Magleby 1995, 38–39, citing Smith and Townsend 1980, 22)

Providing voters with information pamphlets to help explain ballots has not met with great success either, since no one reads them. This renders voters particularly susceptible to the mass media, usually by moneyed interests.

In the deliberative bodies of the popular assemblies, sound-bites would be scrutinized. And advertising aimed at the mass public will always come shy of its target because efforts to reach the randomly selected jury members will always be unlikely at best. Demagogues who whip the masses into a froth might still be able to get items on the agenda in this possible world, but proposed policies would still have to pass deliberative scrutiny to get enacted popularly. The proposal here is aimed at forcing Americans to be more responsible with direct democracy, so that they might have a better chance of enjoying its fruits and legitimating its politics.

The judiciary could, on this model, make sure that the findings of the deliberative bodies cohere with the standards of "equal protection" in some substantial fashion. Since the actual deliberations would be preserved in transcripts (anonymously to protect privacy), judges would have access to the thought processes of the relevant voters. In many cases of judicial review of direct democracy, judges try to infer what the voters must have been thinking when they cast their ballots on a statute that they most likely could not possibly have comprehended. In the case of judicial review of deliberative assemblies, however, judges would have transcripts to facilitate understanding more clearly the preferences of the "lawmakers." And administering post-deliberation surveys would help get more direct statements of the "intentions of the lawmakers."[10]

Justices could still uphold basic constitutional provisions to avert tyranny of the majority and unacceptable deliberative findings. Instead of making the

10. Cohen and Sabel (1997, 337) also rely on this advantage of deliberative assemblies.

circular argument that all good procedures will produce fair results (Habermas 1996; Traub 1996–97, 112–14), I appreciate the concern of the critics of deliberative democracy who rightly fear that, in practice, deliberation will often produce illiberal and "undemocratic" outcomes that might further entrench already inegalitarian power relations. To be sure, this has been a problem with direct democracy in general, but I believe that the institutional mechanisms we already have in place would curb, or at least work against, such outcomes. Yet the benefits of a better approximation of legitimacy suggest strongly deliberative input. While I am not idealizing deliberation as the *only* source of legitimacy (see Chapter 2), I think I am on strong grounds for demanding it.

But judicial opinions, while continuing their Herculean task of checking tyrannical majorities, would also be subject to some popular constraints.[11] The courts would not be able to base their opinions on some tendentious assessment of popular will without actually gauging popular support in a deliberative body. Judiciaries could also call for deliberative juries at state and national levels, especially if they want to adhere to some of Richard Posner's (1999) enthusiasm for social science in judicial decision-making. Indeed, they should be so required if they want to base a decision upon something "deeply rooted in this Nation's . . . tradition."[12] Traditions, particularly "national" ones, would be perfect topics for deliberative control; it seems obvious that the people are particularly well situated to testify to and contest their traditions. Constituting a people should not be a top-down affair.

COMPULSORY SERVICE

I would expect service in deliberative bodies at both local and federal levels to be compulsory civic responsibilities, just as our society expects jury service of

---

11. Habermas, though critiquing Ronald Dworkin for his use of the Herculean judge in a hardly more responsible fashion than the Critical Legal Studies scholars Dworkin criticizes, still seems slightly too judge-centric (Habermas 1996, 211–22).

Alas, Habermas never makes the kind of "nuts and bolts" recommendations I do here to allow the norm of discourse to trickle down into the sphere of popular will-formation. Instead, Habermas thinks deliberative democracy at the level of the judiciary is almost enough to guarantee equal concern and respect. As long as judges take account of what they think each citizen would say if each citizen had access to the forms of discourse, Habermas is willing to compromise and let a liberal constitutional democracy pass discourse-theoretic muster. I doubt we can be this complacent.

12. *Bowers v. Hardwick,* 478 U.S. 186, 192 (1986) (quoting *Moore v. East Cleveland,* 431 U.S. 494, 503 [1977]); see also *Lochner v. New York,* 198 U.S. 45, 76 (1905) (Holmes, J., dissenting: "The statute proposed would infringe fundamental principles as they have been understood by the traditions of our people and our law").

its citizenry. But the legal mandate to participate in deliberative bodies would be far more involved and involving than jury duty: endless deferments and excuses could not be tolerated. Anyone *eligible* to vote should be eligible to be conscripted for a deliberative assembly. Providing translation services for citizens who do not speak English, a reasonable stipend, and traveling expenses, would maximize response rates. Because the voluntary response problem is usually considered one of the most damning shortcomings of deliberative models and referendums,[13] mandatory service—maybe not jail time, but serious repercussions in the form of fines or community service—could avoid that route of delegitimizing the popular forum.

Moreover, mandatory service on policy juries could become a feature constitutive of American citizenship in an age where there are few aspects of political culture that unify citizens. By stigmatizing the act of not serving, by creating a political culture wherein actual citizens are called upon to make decisions that impact their lives in extraordinary ways, the costs of not taking part could become rather severe in civil society. But this is more sociological speculation than argument.

THE END OF TACIT CONSENT

Since it may be that the aggregation of commodified private votes can never amount to consent (including the tacit sort we have grown so reliant upon), I have oriented my proposal to address this democratic dilemma. Yet I substitute a random sample for the population and still expect each deliberator to cast a vote in private. Nevertheless, the deliberations should remain public; the deliberations would be recorded and transcribed to create a public document reporting not only the final vote tally but also what was said at the assembly.

Since each affected person *could* have been selected for the relevant deliberative body, and each person *will* be drafted to serve multiple times in a lifetime, consent is generally made more explicit (and draft-dodgers would have to accept the decisions of the juries because they affirmatively refuse to be decision-makers, not merely a negligible vote). Substantive representation is

13. Turnouts for special elections for ballot initiatives are stunningly low. And those who do turn out are "better educated, older, better off, and more ideological than voters in general elections" (Magleby 1995, 32). For more on why direct democracy cannot be trusted (giving further reasoning for the approach taken here), see Clark 1998. Fishkin supposes that he circumvents the problem with stratified random samples that are representative of the public at large with respect to demographics and preferences, but he, too, experiences the voluntary response problem (Fishkin 1991, 81–104).

more likely to be achieved in this paradigm than it is in our current representative regime, where criteria for representation must always be formalistic or substitutional. Because the institutionalized bargaining function of representatives that often skews representativeness is largely absent from my deliberative institution, citizens can decide for themselves what is worth compromising. But the problems with representation are hardly definitively solved. I am only hoping to do better than we currently do in the quest of achieving the political ends that a thoughtful group would endorse.

AGGREGATION AND DECISION PROCEDURES

Though deliberation is the primary form of decision-making in my model, an aggregating procedure will be necessary at the conclusion of the deliberations because I am concerned with popular will–formation, not only public opinion. Since all deliberative assemblies would be convened to decide binary questions (i.e., yes/no on some proposition), a simple mechanism necessitating a supermajority could be applied to each situation:[14] After deliberation, a private vote is taken where jurors vote "yes," "no," or "abstain." If a two-thirds majority vote "yes" (of those voting "yes" or "no"), the bill under consideration would pass. If a three-fifths majority obtains, shy of two-thirds, I would call the jury hung, keeping the question on the popular agenda for further deliberative assemblies to adjudicate.

Should the jury be hung in the first iteration, those sponsoring the campaign would be entitled to amend their proposition according to the feedback of the first jury. Since the jury's deliberations would be publicly available, the sponsors could tailor their proposal to the needs of the randomly selected jury even though a different jury would be responsible for further consideration of the proposal. The commission would make sure that the changes are reasonable and represent modification on the basis of pervasive comments that come from the deliberators themselves. In any event, three mistrials (hung juries) on any proposition would kill the bill. Of course, if neither a three-fifths supermajority nor a majority is achieved, the measure officially fails and is taken off the deliberative agenda, even supposing that a simple majority might serve as a recommendation to the parties to adopt similar measures by traditional means.

If the proposition came from the people with an initiative-style campaign, it should not come before the branch by this mechanism for three years. Still,

14. A detailed defense for supermajority requirements can be found in Dennis Mueller's work (e.g., Mueller 1996, 180–87). I treat the issue at greater length in Chapter 5.

during this three-year period, a legislature or judiciary could demand popular input on a similar question. If a question is put before the popular assembly by legislators, they would not be able to bring a substantially similar measure within three years either, though an initiative campaign or a judiciary could get a substantially similar measure before the popular branch during the same period. For more details about the proposed system of checks and balances, with more attention to ratification and veto powers, turn to Chapter 4.

AGENDA-SETTING

Of course it would not make sense to have deliberative assemblies set the agenda for other deliberative juries because of the regress problem. Hence, I still need some of the basic mechanisms in place that currently allow for initiatives to be brought before the public. Most often, advocates of a proposal need collect the signatures of a small percentage of the population at issue. Those signatures are sometimes checked for corruption, and the proposal is guided by some basic constraints of wording and reasonable procedural constraints, like subject-matter jurisdiction (Magleby 1995, 25).[15] Alternatively, legislatures or appellate judiciaries could decide to put questions on the agenda.

In Chapter 7, I tackle the most difficult and central problem of agenda-setting and framing. As a teaser, I think there are two approaches to this challenge: one concrete and the other more theoretical. The concrete approach suggests that candidates in general elections may, given this reconstituted regime, start running on the basis of the questions they want to submit to the popular branch. In this way, citizens will have some access to the referendum (as opposed to the initiative) agenda-setters. Of course, I could not *require* candidates to have their platforms include what they will put to juries to decide (since it would rarely be in the hands of a single legislator to draw up an issue for the popular agenda). But empirical evidence suggests that candidates in states that make wide use of the referendum often run on platforms that endorse facilitation of public decision-making on various items of interest to the candidates and the public (Magleby 1995, 29).

15. "Subjects excluded from the ballot in some states include naming a person to office by initiative, emergency legislation, and using the referendum to block appropriations. Some states 'require that a measure may not encompass more than a single subject'" (Magleby 1995, 25, citing California Constitution, Art. II, § 8 [d]; Florida Constitution, Art. XI, § 3; Oregon Constitution, Art. IV, § 1[2][d]). These seem like reasonable and necessary procedural means to help measures of direct democracy function more efficiently—and may make elites more likely to trust my proposal in general.

The theoretical approach is a form of "the civil society argument"—citizens, in their civil associations, their smaller public spheres, will frame issues themselves for the use of the larger political public sphere. A radical shift in how campaign funds are appropriated could facilitate this process by adopting Fishkin's (1991, 99–100) sketch of a voucher system, elaborated upon in Bruce Ackerman's (1993, 71–80) "Patriot Proposal," wherein every citizen could allocate some public funds to the interest group of his or her choice. In Chapter 7, I use these reform efforts to gesture toward my own mechanism. In the meantime, if and when civil society fails us, we will just have to trust our representatives (both elected officials and those randomly selected for the popular branch) to do a reasonable job of presenting as many alternatives and arguments as possible, forcing them to employ nonpartisan help (the CCCA-like entity adumbrated above) in arbitrating between partisan arguments. The anti-utopian institution tinkerer always uses the shadow of the present situation to gauge progress.

BRANCHES

This scheme very much relies on the interaction of the various branches.[16] Surely, one cannot depend upon deliberation for all our "democratic" decisions. We must often leave it to other features of institutional design in other branches to enact the virtues of "political equality" and "nontyranny." Thus, I have no reason to do away with general elections, courts, and administrative bodies; I need them to continue their administrative, oversight, legislative, statute-tailoring, and interpretive activities. Every citizen could not be expected to gain expertise in lawmaking, nor should it be desirable that they spend much of their time doing so. Thus, I would imagine that the construction of the fine details of obscure code would still be left in the hands of the legislatures and agencies. To protect against tyranny of the majority, the judiciary would still have a substantial role in such a government to prevent abuses of the popular branch. Just as referendums have had illiberal outcomes in the past, we should reasonably fear that deliberative bodies will make some bad

16. Fishkin does not give enough attention to the value of the separation of powers in his work. This shortcoming inspires my proposal's excessive fixation on it. In Chapters 3 and 4, I spell out more explicitly these sorts of considerations. The insight here is that we can trust direct democracy if we have the right checks in place. Instead of doing away with direct democracy and depending solely upon representation or judicial review, we can have a branch that really includes independent individuals coming together to make law.

decisions. But judicial review of even this form of direct democracy is not entirely inappropriate, and it should be welcomed in our attempt to balance republicanism and liberalism, popular rule and avoidance of a tyrannous majority.[17] Though the executive (the president or governors) and a super-majority of the relevant legislatures should be "allowed" to repeal or veto laws enacted by deliberative assemblies, such action is likely to be political suicide, if not perceived as authoritarian. But judges sometimes need to take the lead and be "undemocratic" in extraordinary circumstances. Similarly, the popular branch could check some judicial abuses as well by contesting "general will" claims that occasionally appear in judicial decisions as a basis for deciding law; instead, judges would have to call for a deliberative jury to assess popular will. Because I wish to avoid infinite regress on the one hand, and inattention to redressing discrimination on the other, my institutional reform proposal does not take the form of a radical overthrow of our current system. Nonetheless, real changes are needed if popular sovereignty is to be taken sufficiently seriously.

MORE DETAILS

Let me summarize five salient features of Fishkin's model (and my departures therefrom) that I would want to see used as a basis for the mechanical imple-mentation of my proposal.

Selecting Participants

The citizen juries are stratified random samples, chosen with a view toward getting a broadly representative sample of the population at large. Of course, the most immediate questions are: "Representative of whom more specifically?" "Can I allow race-based representation? Class-based? Occupation-based?" "Does strict demographic mirroring satisfy the demands of scientific represen-tativeness?" "Why shouldn't I embrace the jury model, which depends to a far greater extent on lotteries than on statistical sampling, which may further entrench suspect classifications like race and gender?" "Do I really think twelve percent of my participants being black can sufficiently account for represent-ing black interests?" These are powerful questions (that are treated at length in their own literatures) that do not yield obvious answers.

17. Julian Eule (1990) argues that any form of direct democracy deserves a hard judicial look. For more on the check of judicial review upon the popular branch, see Chapter 4.

As a general rule, however, Fishkin's sampling does quite well against these sorts of objections because his samples tend to reproduce initial preferences and demographic indicators in the larger pool of public opinion. He demonstrates that his samples do generally reflect the diversity of perspectives in society as a whole. To be sure, I am not sure we can settle the matter as a question of normative political theory: no theory of representation will provide clear answers as to how to go about this task. But institutionally, my general reform could probably effect some progress over current representative regimes in terms of representation of minority interests regardless of the method I ultimately select.[18] In any event, it may simply be true that there is no preformed political will that needs representation. Providing the opportunities for deliberative assemblies is a way to create informed political will. And representativeness results, not because of *who* is included, but because of *how* individuals are included. Deliberation without the prospect for bargaining forces a particular sort of attention to the question at hand. Using geographically stratified random samples is the most obvious content-neutral and viewpoint-neutral method of selecting jurors.

Nonetheless, the problem of self-selection for Fishkin is as problematic as he claims it is for town-hall meetings and call-in broadcasts. Asking subjects to submit to deliberative assemblies is intimidating and time-intensive. The kind of people who would agree to expose themselves to a weekend of arguing surely causes a voluntary response problem. My mandating participation (see Chapter 6 for the targeted argument) skirts this problem. Even Fishkin (1991, 9), in his less cautious moments, writes that the "role of delegate should be considered analogous to that of juror. If this kind of event were eventually institutionalized, it should come to be considered an obligation of citizenship." A most suggestive gesture indeed.

My selection process would be just as careful as Fishkin's, and I would recommend administering a predeliberative questionnaire, not to see if people change their minds after deliberation as Fishkin does (by now we know people do), but to help ensure that a still content-neutral diversity of perspectives are heard. Discussion in each of the smaller groups should go in different directions even if the CCCA-like agency could not plan the exact representation in the smaller group, thereby having too much substantive input on the

18. Magleby (1995, 44, citing Baker 1991, 710) reports: "Lynn Baker has used public choice theory to explore the question of whether minorities do better in representative institutions than in direct democracy. She refutes 'the claims that racial minorities are better served by representative than direct law-making processes' and urges minorities to focus on ways to improve direct democracy rather than abolish it."

direction of the deliberations. Democratic practice in the public sphere must depend upon exposure to some diversity of perspective and some expressions of self-interest, even if enlightened. Though some minimalist versions of democracy might cast it as a procedural practice that allows private voting without discussion and majoritarian rule, surely a "strong" democracy must demand more. The private vote was instituted to cure certain ills with the public vote, which was the better theoretically grounded mechanism. But the private vote has pathologies of its own: it shields citizens from one another and commodifies votes. The popular branch is the necessary corrective, because often seeing and hearing a person expressing his or her own self-interest and its back story is a way to change a mind. Democracies must allow (and even provide for) the capacity of the citizens to change their minds; that is its progressive and experimental strain.

Competence and Moderating It

Fishkin's model also addresses "citizen competence" (Fishkin and Luskin 1999, 7; see generally Elkin and Edwards 1999). The critics of deliberative democracy rightly emphasize the degree to which citizens know very little and are prone to defer to experts or just yell unproductively at one another, given the opportunity (Button and Mattson 1999). But this is no excuse for paternalism.

Fishkin puts his best foot forward, not only by taking an "educative" stance in helping citizens work through the issues with pamphlets and videos,[19] but also by encouraging participation and carefully training moderators in social psychology such that they do not let the big-mouths rule the floor. In his polls, "80% of the participants spoke," "note-taking was common," and "incivilities were rare" (Fishkin and Luskin 1999, 12).[20] Of course, critics of democracy throughout the ages have stressed the degree to which democracy must be a

---

19. The educational pamphlets in many states have not been a great success, but I (unsurprisingly) think it relates to the fact that voters still have incentives for ignorance—this is the well-known "rational ignorance problem." Flicking a lever one way or the other is simply easier than wading through hundreds of pages of explanation. My more deliberative regime heightens expectations and incentives. Fishkin has noted that participants often become much more engaged in politics in general when they know that they will be part of his Deliberative Polls. *A fortiori*, I expect this reaction when their $1/n$ vote becomes a substantial piece of the pie ($1/525$, with an opportunity to convince fourteen others) and not an infinitesimal one, and their vote is expression of a will, not merely an opinion.

20. Since Fishkin's polls are not compulsory, he likely gets a large number of talkers; the voluntary response problem suggests that he would be likely to attract the talkative ones.

rule by demagogues. But those who run the Deliberative Polls are taught how to diminish the effects of such a tendency. The moderators are, after all, selected for their fairness and impartiality.

This suggests that we should perhaps recruit federal judges to moderate as long as they undergo training by social psychologists to learn how to control anyone trying to monopolize the discourse (though I imagine they have most of the relevant training already). Even if a particular judge's track record suggests partiality on a specific issue, most judges would be usable as moderators who settle only questions of fact and decorum. The moderators should be able to settle questions of fact for the jurors to help them in their deliberations, since many preferences are obviously based on misinformation and misleading statistics. Since the transcripts would be public, judges would not be able to get away with steering conversation subtly. Impartiality will always be imperfect, but this proposal is less imperfect than an oligarchy where only moneyed voices rule and interest groups are the only political force acting against politicians' self-interest in preserving an overclass to reelect them.

In a recent Deliberative Poll I helped organize in New Haven, we used volunteers from the Connecticut League of Women Voters as our moderators; they were competent and helped ensure maximal participation from our deliberators, who themselves amazed us with their ability to process and analyze complicated policy questions.

Breaking Up the People to Get the Voice of the People

The discussions would take place in small groups of fifteen people with thirty-five going on at once in the same location, all facilitated by moderators. To be sure, the basic briefing about the proposal and its history could take place in a plenary session led by politicians or administrators, but the deliberations proper would be done on the micro level. This ensures that different routes of conversation are explored and addresses Dahl's (1970, 54, 118; Dahl and Tufte 1973) insight that there are "upper limits" to effective participation. Dahl estimates that six hundred people can be part of a general deliberative body, not so different from the number proposed here. Surely, real discourse requires small sets of individuals, rendering undesirable both Dahl's "minipopulus" and deLeon's "PPA" of one thousand participants. It also suggests that the fad of arguing for electronic deliberation is mostly cyberblather: who ever reads their mail from subscribed lists, especially those with a thousand subscribers?

Doctrine of Affected Interests

All "stakeholder groups" affected by deliberation should be allowed access to sway the direction of the body's deliberations. Of course, this is a rather tricky condition because just who counts as a stakeholder will always be in the hands of administrators (and civil society as explored in Chapter 7). But even supposing an imperfect administration, we can imagine that many different perspectives could be considered over the course of a few days. One way to address this particular concern would be to adopt a voucher scheme, where all citizens (not only those selected for deliberation) get credits to allocate money toward interest groups, providing extra help to the major advocates and independents looking to publicize and organize their efforts. But most important, unlike Fishkin's polls, I emphasize that agenda-setting cannot be solely in the hands of elites.

No Gagging

Finally, I would be very hesitant to impose "gag rules" at the deliberations (Holmes 1993a). Jon Elster (1998, 16) notes that "an attempt to take an issue off the agenda is likely to place it even more firmly on the agenda."[21] Moreover, what Fishkin's work shows is that such rules are not necessary—people can have fruitful dialogue without rigorous gag rules. As Elster (1998, 100) argues, "The mere fact that an assembly of individuals defines its task as that of deliberation rather than mere force-based bargaining exercises a powerful influence on the proposals and arguments that can be made." While people like Ackerman and Habermas might aim for "constrained conversation," allowing for the admission of only the "Rational" or the "Public-Spirited" in debate, I would remain suspicious of such efforts; I explain why in the next chapter.

In general, the attempt to police what people say in public forums is not only unlikely to succeed anywhere off of a spaceship with a high commander (Ackerman 1980), but is also probably undesirable. Why force someone to lie in public if his or her opposition to same-sex marriage is biblically inspired? Why not just push the person through deliberation to question whether her biblical commitments are relevant to the political question? Failure to change someone's ideological commitments is not devastating. Failure to try by shutting out the religious from the political public sphere is not only revolting, but also stands in the way of progress and truly altering preferences because it incentivizes preference-falsification (Kuran 1995).

21. For more on how gag rules in these kinds of forums tend to be counterproductive empirically, Elster recommends looking at Miller 1999.

SUMMING UP

Habermas appreciates the need for postmetaphysical thinking and believes we have little choice but to embrace such modes of argumentation "for which no plausible alternatives exist" (Habermas 1996, 443). The proposal at issue is not only realistic, but also has the capacity to transform our society in such a way that would satisfy liberals and communitarians, consensus theorists and agonistic political philosophers alike. It is realistic because our political climate could absorb and afford such an institutional reorganization. It requires a reshuffling of resources, but not total redistribution of wealth, a reassessing of the implications of our form of government, but not a reconsideration of whether democracy is the best form of government. While it challenges our assumptions about what it means to endorse "representative" government, the proposal does not call for undisciplined populist direct democracy. It is anti-utopian because it only hopes to approximate an approximation some-what better. It does not require assent to some grand narrative other than our weak (or "thin") democratic one, where the people should actually have some input on a level more informed and less economically determined than the initiative and referendum of our current representative regime. It is a practical way to make us feel more at home under our laws, which would be rendered more democratic if subjected to the new branch of government I recommend. Though I suffer from acute "polis envy,"[22] I do not view this as a foolhardy malady; many real ills and pathologies can be treated with a dose of delibera-tion. The problem requires clever institutional design, even though I may fail to persuade that my particular design is clever enough.

The proposal takes seriously both the ideals of individuality and individual interests, and the politics of difference and group interests, though I will not be able to spell out all of these advantages in this context. By finding a place for procedural justice, and taking the civil society argument into account so that the state does not have a monopoly on agenda-setting (Chapter 7), the proposal addresses a variety of liberal and communitarian concerns, all while avoiding making difficult fundamental-rights arguments for equality. Such arguments shall be left to the theorists and the jurists (even the jurors!) as I try to argue for a practical proposal to embody a dominant theme of Amer-ican democratic life that might support such a reform.[23] No doubt, such a

22. I take the term from Fishkin (1991, 90), but he credits Bruce Ackerman with coining it. John McCormick claims that Stephen Holmes should get credit.

23. Here is the empirical support for the democratic climate to which I am appealing: "Depending on the precise wording of the question, more than 50 percent of Americans support

proposal rests on foundational ideas insofar as it will need a theory of why governmental institutions should preserve equality and facilitate heightened degrees of self-government. I do not make such an argument here because though the terms of what counts for equality are still on the table, that our equality should be protected does not seem very controversial. And though the terms of how directly the people should influence policy are still up for debate, it seems uncontroversial that the realities of money and power often undo even a trace of self-governance.

---

the idea of national referenda [to supplant Congress and the President in making certain categories of national decisions] and more than 80 percent support both the initiative and the recall" of congressmen and senators once they have been in office for a year (King 1997). These numbers are more recent than, though corroborate similar findings and enthusiasm evidenced in, Thomas E. Cronin's (1989, 223–34) pioneering work.

2

ARGUING FOR ARGUING

Each theory of deliberative democracy must and should posit an answer to at least two questions: how should we deliberate, and why should we deliberate? There is no consensus about the answers to either of these questions—one might say there is vigorous agonism and contestation about it.

Basically, there are two models for how we should deliberate: the elitist/liberal and the populist/democratic. Of course, we can also imagine some combination of or compromise as we settle on a dualist, or two-track, model. In the elitist camp are those who depend primarily on the judiciary or legislative branches to deliberate, thinking that elites serving as trustees or protectors can do the job just fine. Many political liberals and proceduralists (e.g., Rawls 1996) fall in this camp, since they look to the courts to tell us what we would think under the right conditions and using the best procedures. Perhaps another elitist theory is Waldron's (1999) attempt to think about deliberation in the context of legislation in his *Dignity of Legislation*.

And why shouldn't the elitists also invoke the founders? Indeed, representative government seems to have been designed with this function in mind. The Federalist argument for representation is rather simple: James Madison wanted "to refine and enlarge the public views by passing them through the medium of a . . . body of citizens" (Kramnick 1987, 126). Also, Alexander Hamilton saw the representative body as an "opportunity for cool and sedate reflection" (410).

The elitist version of deliberative democracy receives a definitive justification from John Stuart Mill (1993, 335): "Everyone has a right to feel insulted by being made a nobody, and stamped as of no account at all. No one but a fool . . . feels offended by the acknowledgment that there are others whose opinion, and even whose wish, is entitled to a greater amount of consideration than his."

A proper conception of democracy sensitive to the goal of popular sovereignty, however, must demand more than legislative bodies taking part in mostly nondeliberative bargaining. Access to "representative" bodies is usually limited to a group of elites whose primary interests are fund-raising and interest-group pandering. While "critics of [a more deliberative regime] tend to argue that nondeliberative processes might approximate the judgments people would reach with fuller information and reflection—and save everyone decision costs through the use of heuristics," James Fishkin's evidence nearly proves that "heuristics or shortcuts [cannot] plausibly proxy for deliberation" (Fishkin 1999a, 2–3; 1997, 205–9, 214–20; Fishkin and Luskin 1999, 14–29). I cannot possibly survey Fishkin's evidence in this context, but I do assume that it bears out the claim that ordinary citizens change their minds as a result of deliberation and that there is no shortcut to figuring out just how conversation will change people's minds.[1] Moreover, pragmatically speaking, people may be more likely to view decisions made in a deliberative body that is composed more popularly as having more legitimacy than any heuristic. Given such a condition, there is no good reason to avoid conversation with actual citizens, when it can, not only inspire more democratic governance, but also inculcate the kind of civic virtue so many political theorists (e.g., Sandel 1996) argue is useful to counteract the pathologies of individualism that mass democracy induces.

Though Habermas (1996) is generally associated with a two-track model, his version of deliberative democracy does not develop the institutional potential for an organized populist component. He often too hopefully leaves the legal community to perform integration functions on its own. He succumbs to elitism especially when Rawls (1996) backs him into a corner calling the "ideal speech

---

1. For further evidence, see Button and Mattson 1999 and Neblo 1999. Neblo's evidence seems to suggest that deliberation produces moderate or compromise outcomes; much of that has to do with his experimental design, discussed elsewhere in this book. What Fishkin's experiments show is not only that a random sample of individuals can mirror the population's views at large, but that minds (in statistically significant numbers) are changed in the process. Whereas Fishkin and Luskin's work show deliberation as effecting unpredictable outcomes, Neblo's work suggests that deliberative situations do tend to produce outcomes with more "generalizability." Nonetheless, in either case, deliberative input provides normative advantages, so a tendency toward certain outcomes may not ultimately disturb us: the virtues of civic republicanism here can outweigh a possible detectable predictability in deliberative outcomes.

situation" a "device of representation." His further retreat into Madisonianism finds him too sanguine about the status quo, never letting deliberative democracy touch the lives of nonpolitical individuals, never letting the citizens do any of the talking, rarely letting the concerns of the periphery to get to the core. Indeed, the elitists are often rightfully concerned with outcomes and not procedures proper. But the fixation on outcomes tends to devolve into a form of paternalism, which is precisely what makes the elitist theories disturbing. While we can let Habermas call himself a proceduralist if we are in a generous mood, his paradigm of law is principally concerned with substantive outcomes. To be sure, Habermas would not leave democratic procedures as they are in his effort to let only public reasons count, but he is more liberal in allowing heuristics and proxies to do the work of legitimation. Let us at least note that elitists may be subject to the countermajoritarian difficulty when they offer the policies of the few to stand for the deliberation of the many. Isn't rule by the few over the many one condition institutionalized deliberation may be poised to ameliorate?

Sabel and Cohen (2002), in their effort to describe the contours of "sovereignty and solidarity in the EU," have much more populist/democratic ideas about how we should deliberate. Though they are satisfied to see deliberation as an emerging *fact* of EU integration (operating through the new federalisms), they are far less engaged in offering normative work with attention to how Americans can make their regime more deliberative. Populist deliberative democrats find themselves more concerned with the people themselves, not their representatives or judges. Instead, populists focus attention on citizens' *recognition* of one another and the re-cognition of the public sphere, made possible through contestatory deliberative interactions among lay citizens. Endemic to this priority is often a concentration on contestation and agonism because peoples' identities, opaque as they may be, are often at stake. While elites can also engender contestation, it is nevertheless true that the populists are more likely to heed the contests going on at the periphery, voices that have not yet established elites that represent their interests in elite political institutions. This is the model endorsed here—an agonistic populist deliberative democracy, where deliberators are conscripted and paid in order to incentivize as many clashing voices as possible to constitute the civic voice.

But even the agonistic populists spend most of their time deconstructing the public sphere, not reconfiguring it with practical reform proposals. The failures of voluntary associations and town meetings are apparent; the educative effects of populism are unproven and will suffer from the voluntary response problem; the therapy deliberative democracy can offer leaves us with many pathologies that should keep us awake at night, especially because many are returns of the repressed—we opt for representation and deliberative decision-making to avoid many of the pathologies of plebiscitary democracy. Design is the task at hand.

As must be obvious by now, it is difficult to disentangle the how of deliberation from the why because there are interaction effects. Deliberation may be an end in itself: the people who believe this are often delighted to see it instantiated everywhere. If it is good for moral edification and therapy, it isn't surprising that Barber's (1984) romanticism is confusingly all-encompassing and too strong. If we believe in the doctrine of the wisdom of the multitude with Aristotle, deliberation is set up as a means toward wisdom. But, as Aristotle insists, wisdom may be an aristocratic virtue, so keeping deliberative democracy safe in elitist representative bodies could be well-advised even if not particularly democratic. If it is a means toward Pareto-optimal resource allocation, we will see some wavering about whether representation is acceptable. If it is supposed to educate citizens or to inculcate largess, then populism may be the only option.

In any case, Elster (1998, 11) gives us a catalog of what deliberation may be good for: deliberation "reveals private information; lessens or overcomes the impact of bounded rationality; forces or induces a particular mode of justifying demands; legitimizes the ultimate choice; is desirable for its own sake; makes for Pareto-superior decisions; makes for better decisions in terms of distributive justice; makes for larger consensus; [and] improves the moral or intellectual qualities of the participants."

With all these advantages, who would want to be against it? And once it is desired, any theory of deliberative democracy should take a stand on the how and the why of deliberation, even if one ultimately chooses a compound of various procedures and justifications.

As I explained in the Introduction, the primary answer I offer to the question of "why deliberation" for my model of deliberative democracy here is to cure legitimacy deficits. We can pursue the other worthwhile goals and reform efforts adumbrated in the Introduction, but it may be that deliberative democracy is just not worth the effort without tying it to a theory of how it affords greater legitimacy. Of course, there is very little cost to wasting paper explaining how we already have a deliberative democracy and letting the naysayers doubt whether such is actually the case, which, of course, it is not. But Habermas started the deliberative democracy business as its own enterprise, and the whole point of the discourse theory of law really is to cure legitimacy deficits. We can be content with the approximation political liberal institutions afford, or we can be slightly more utopian and come up with some real populist modes of bringing about its realization. Unfortunately, the two-track dualisms of people like Ackerman (1991; 1980), Habermas (1996), and Benhabib (2002) tend to let law spend too much time taking care of itself in normal politics, when they obviously agree that legitimacy rests with popular sovereignty, a product of what Ackerman would call revolutionary politics. But normal politics must be sensitive to the murmurings of paradigm shifts going on at the periphery that have not yet mobilized or politicized themselves to speak in the language familiar at the core, where the work of deliberation seems to take place for the dualists. Agonistic populist deliberative democrats like myself make efforts to find mechanisms to render the core more porous and less controlled by forms of elite rationality.

THE VERSION OF DELIBERATIVE DEMOCRACY EMBRACED HERE

So what model of deliberative democracy do I embrace here? I have suggested that I prefer populism to elitism and believe that we should deliberate to cure legitimacy deficits, but I can say more to situate my model.

For one, Habermas's version is occasionally too strong for my taste. He writes, "Only those statutes may claim legitimacy that can meet with the assent of all citizens in a discursive process" (Habermas 1996, 110). Instead, I appeal to Fishkin's (1991, 3) intuitive suggestion that it is a "false dilemma" to suppose "that we must choose between thoughtful but anti-democratic competence of elites on the one hand, and the superficialities of mass democracy on the other." Though Fishkin's proposals for reform are too mild to address balancing his trilemma of "political equality, tyranny of the majority, and deliberation" (1991, 12), I take the urgency of his construction to heart. His problematization begs for a firm institutional role for deliberative processes, even if Madisonian representative government must *also* play a role, in spite of its failure to achieve deliberative decision-making. As I have already suggested, my point of departure is Fishkin's series of experiments with Deliberative Polling.

Habermas (1996, 362) writes, "Political opinion polls provide a certain reflection of 'public opinion' only if they have been preceded by a focused public debate and a corresponding opinion-formation in a mobilized public sphere." He thinks we can only talk about "preferences" as what one "would express after weighing the relevant information and arguments" (336). Addressing this criterion, Fishkin (1991, 1) invented his Deliberative Polls: "A deliberative opinion poll models what the public *would* think, if it had a more adequate chance to think about the questions at issue." By taking seriously the extent to which the voting public is uninformed and unreflective, Fishkin aims to create a deliberative situation to cure these pathologies of mass democracy. In his experimental setup, a small group of citizens is selected by stratified random sample and brought together to deliberate about a given set of policy questions in a jury-like setting. It is provided with informational materials and treated to a short retreat with plenary sessions led by politicians. The participants' preferences are tracked over the course of the deliberations to see how exposure to deliberation alters citizens' preferences.

"Deliberative polling is valuable precisely because it presents the voice not of experts or pundits but of the people. And not as they are, but as they would be, having learned more about the issues and had the opportunity of coming to a considered judgment about them" (Fishkin and Luskin 1999, 6). Thus, "the ultimate point of such a poll is prescriptive, not predictive. Its results have prescriptive force because they are the voice of the people under special conditions where the people have had a chance to think about the issues and hence should have a voice worth listening to" (Fishkin 1991, 4). The primary task of the body is to arrive at an independent decision (not a consensus), keeping public concerns in mind while addressing individuals' private preferences. By undergoing this kind of activity, not only do the participants become more informed, but they also take more seriously their role in public affairs more generally.[2] To be sure, there will be questions for which experts will need to provide input. But the basic point is that there are too many questions that are left in the hands of unaccountable judges and other elites that the people are competent to answer. Democracy should tend to prefer some organized and thoughtful voice of the people, even if constraints will be necessary to ensure that democracy can be trusted. Constraint is one of the reasons for the separation of powers in the first place, and the people ought to have a voice of their own, to have a power all their own, one that need not partake of the bargaining so common in the current representative system. As I hope to show in the next two chapters, the separation of powers is exactly what will enable us to imagine a future for democracy that is more or less consistent with our current representative regime, but is much more legitimate.

Ultimately, I am more interested in the possibilities for direct democracy than Fishkin. I share the standard suspicions of an excessively plebiscitary model: "It is a dubious accomplishment to give power to the people under conditions where they are not really in a position to think about how they are to exercise that power" (Fishkin 1991, 21). But wide use of Fishkin's procedure to

---

2. This is not just speculation. Both Fishkin and Luskin (1999) and Button and Mattson (1999) show results that bear out the thesis that deliberative situations make citizens more likely to be interested in political affairs.

derive actual policy, not simply to disseminate information and garner public opinion, should allay some of the obvious critiques of the referendum. As much as the hardcore deliberative democrats might protest that every single citizen must take part in the discourses (though they might not—we never really know what sorts of institutions will satisfy the discourse-theoretic appetite), this condition is too unrealistic to take seriously. Surely what it must mean is that every citizen's deliberation must be represented in a nonfictively attributable sense (Michelman 1997); Congress and the Supreme Court are not close enough to the trenches and still leave us with legitimacy deficits. Thus, Fishkin's experiments not only recommend a model for a reasonable approximation of injecting a level of representative deliberation into government; radicalizing his Deliberative Polls to be more institutionally intertwined with political mechanisms might be a good way to bring about some of the goals that deliberative democrats prize: legitimacy and an informed public sphere that can author political discourse.

In the previous chapter, I outlined three major critiques of the standard referendum and initiative processes: (1) their propensity for poor and biased turnout (a form of the voluntary response problem); (2) their unacceptable reliance on moneyed interest groups; and (3) the problem that results from the opacity of the material under consideration. A radicalization (with modifications, like mandatory service) of Fishkin's methods of Deliberative Polling is poised to address each of these problems. First, mandatory service with stratified random sampling addresses the lack of representativeness in direct democracy voters. Furthermore, scrutiny of proposals over the course of a few days ensures getting past sound-bite politics, thereby disempowering the forces swaying voters in expensive media advertising campaigns. Last, plenary informational sessions and research materials, as well as extended exploration in the small groups at the Deliberative Polls (with moderators trained to settle relevant questions of fact), should ensure that people at least comprehend the statutes under consideration. Integrating deliberative assemblies into lawmaking provides an opportunity for citizen input into decision-making processes, without many of the shortcomings of the referendum and the initiative. To be sure, my proposal will leave us with a whole host of problems old and new. My hope is to convince that the trade-off is worthwhile.

Fishkin ultimately suppresses the tremendous potential of the deliberative situation he designs. He exhibits a profound deference to our current modes of representation because he does not trust direct democracy. In the first instance, he only wanted the Deliberative Polls to be "initial evaluations" of potential candidates and was interested in their ability to replace the disproportionate importance of the primary elections in the early states (Fishkin 1991, 8, 96). Concentration on major elections diverts attention from part of the problem: politics will remain spectatorial and voyeuristic as long as citizens see it as a sporting event. If issues and policies are to take center stage, it would be more useful to have citizen debate about those things, not about personalities or parties. This is why particular political personalities should get marginalized in deliberative assemblies as this book envisions them. Personalities and parties get plenty of attention in the other branches, so my inattention to them here should not be seen as an oversight or as closing off of the possibility for politics as usual—or "normal politics" as Ackerman (1991) might have it.

Recently, Deliberative Polls have been organized to tackle local and regional issues as well as national ones, unrelated to any one election or initiative proposal. While these collections of public opinion certainly ought, in the ideal polity, to instruct policymakers about what their constituency would think under more informed conditions and bind them to it, the poll results still have no binding effect and the proposal offered here seeks to make populist deliberative results binding.

Currently, Fishkin relies heavily upon the media to make his polls politically important (Fishkin and Luskin 1999, 5)—recall that Habermas (1996) calls the media a fourth branch. While the media's attention to networks of deliberation is critical, until such time as the polls have direct impact on policy, coverage will only be possible on public television. Results of a nationally binding deliberative assembly on same-sex marriage would run simultaneously on all three major networks, much the way the State of the Union address does.[3]

The Jefferson Center for New Democratic Processes in Minnesota has proposed and experimented with electoral juries of twelve to eighteen people who monitor presidential campaigns to make public recommendations. They have also experimented with "policy juries" that have grappled with such issues as the ethics of organ transplants (Fishkin 1997, 97).[4] I think that these gestures are very hopeful and that we should continue to look at what these juries decide so that we can convince ourselves that laypersons can be trusted to rule themselves

3. Of course, citizens not only would be *allowed* to keep their identities private, but all means necessary should be taken to keep them private before and during the days of deliberation to avoid the danger of their being manipulated, bribed, or bombarded by interest-group or corporate haranguing and electioneering. For more on the difficulties of privacy and publicity, see Chapter 5.

4. Ned Crosby, the head of the Jefferson Center, has reported on a wide range of experiments, which I discuss in Chapters 1 and 6.

in a larger measure than they do now.[5] But none of these *experimental* situations has its eye on the prize. I want to radicalize the use of these units and have them engaged in actual institutionalized decision-making about *policies,* not about *politics.* Until they are so engaged, they will embody many of the pathologies of deliberation (like deference to experts) without providing for any of the benefits (like more legitimacy and more civic virtue). To employ a Habermasian distinction, in a functioning republic, "opinion-formation" is only one aspect that lawmaking needs to be attentive to. For law to emanate from the civic voice of the people, nonfictive "will-formation" should be central. The way of achieving nonfictive will-formation is through populist deliberative procedures aimed at forming a will instead of an opinion.[6]

Fishkin (1991, 37) is correct to commend Dahl for getting us thinking about how time will always constrain deliberation. "Time always matters when a decision has to be made" (Elster 1998, 6). So, there is no reason to lament that we will have to vote at the end of the deliberative sessions, something Fishkin tends to want to avoid at his polls. In fact, voting after deliberation makes sense in light of Aristotle's position (1985, 1112a13–1113a15) that deliberation must always be about *doing* something ultimately,[7] something some ideal proceduralists seem to deny in requiring a logically complete argument. And what thinking about time also brings to the foreground is why we should reject Dahl (1970; 1989) and deLeon's (1997) proposed reforms that citizens be enlisted to watch over executive officials, because common sense should

5. On the issue of jury competence, the empirical research and the literature is quite heartening even if many would like to do away with them for normative considerations. Chapter 6 is devoted to the jury and what it can teach us about the uses and disadvantages of deliberation.

6. Bernard Manin (1994) argues that we should depend exclusively on deliberative will-formation as the only source of legitimacy for a republic. I do not follow Manin in his monolithic treatment of deliberation, but it is a very important paper in the literature, and it delivers a very good argument for deliberation's importance in will-formation. It is also sensitive to Habermasian extremes, taking the more reasonable view (against Habermas's seeming need for unanimous consensus in discursive practices) that "given the appropriate procedural rules for deliberation, the better argument is simply the one that generates more support and not the one that is able to convince all participants" (200). But see Mueller 1996, 180–87, in which Mueller argues that if consensus is implausible, the appropriate second-best is attaining a supermajority, not merely a majority. Supermajorities and their role in this proposal are discussed in Chapter 5.

7. Aristotle (1985, 1112a13–1113a15) offers that "by 'open to deliberation,' presumably, we should mean what someone with some sense, not some fool or madman, might deliberate about." Aristotle also argues that "no one deliberates about eternal things . . . rather, we deliberate about what results through our agency . . . where the outcome is unclear and the right way to act is undefined. And we enlist partners in deliberation on large issues when we distrust our own ability to discern [the right answer]. We deliberate not about ends, but about what promotes ends" (1112a23–1112b13).

tell us that it is unreasonable to ask citizens to take a *year* out of their lives to deliberate.

Even Habermas (1996, 340) is aware that "the actual course of [deliberative] debates deviates from the ideal procedure of deliberative politics." In fact, he goes further when he claims that the whole concept of the ideal speech situation is a "methodological fiction": "Even under favorable conditions, no complex society could ever correspond to the model of purely communicative relations" (326). Habermas keeps us talking about ideal conditions, however, because "presuppositions of rational discourse have a steering effect on the course of debate" (340). If this is true, theorists still deserve some attention to help us craft better versions of deliberation. But too often they get caught up worrying about ideal conditions without giving attention to plausible ones that would help them achieve their goal of a more deliberative republic.

Before proceeding to more details about my proposal, I would like briefly to engage a theoretical formulation that seeks to "maxim-ize" deliberation; I wish to try to make realistic some of the ideal conditions about rationality that occasionally do more to constrain deliberation than to steer it. As I hope to demonstrate in this book, the theory of deliberative democracy could be far more valuable if it considered how it could actually be practiced. As Barber (1990, 193) notes: "In conquering the muddled uncertainties of politics and suborning reasonableness to rationality, they [philosophers and ideal discourse theorists] have served the ideal of enlightenment better than they have informed our political judgment."

A TEASPOONFUL OF THEORY TO MAKE THE MEDICINE GO DOWN

Joshua Cohen provides some philosophical tools to ground and better describe a version of deliberative democracy; I shall try to be less foundationalist than he about the role of Reason in such a paradigm to explore how we might imagine a more practical and pragmatic theory of deliberative democracy. Some (including Cohen) think the whole framework of deliberative democracy falls apart without an appeal to a strong notion of rationality. I hope to explore in this digression how we can do without the strong version of the ideal because I am suspicious of Reason's tyranny and its implicit elitism; I do not think we need to be *über*reasoners to make approximately legitimate law in a democracy. Such metanarratives (even the Reason *über alles* story), such versions of the good life, are precisely the kind of talk that people like Ackerman (1980) should not allow in the political public sphere in the first place. Instead, I endorse Habermas's more textured idea of the public sphere, which has room for moral disagreement—and claims of superiority. We should expect and hope to see the irrational voice itself in a public sphere with any vitality. A public sphere with any legitimacy must at least try to recognize people and what is central to their identities, even if it means providing a forum for some to express their (misguided) claims to superiority.

In the first instance, discourse theory is supposed to be postmetaphysical. Thus, Habermas's wavering about whether the people really can be the source of legitimacy, especially if their reasoning and deliberation do not effect rational or perfectly just results, undermines his use of democratic discourse as a legitimator. Here, the faith that perfect institutional procedures will produce perfectly egalitarian results need not bind us: this faith causes headaches for many deliberative democrats who do not want to admit that a perfect procedure without any substance (whatever that might mean) cannot guarantee results. Habermas's criticisms of Cohen will be enough to help us take a stand where Habermas himself wavers. I conclude that populist deliberative procedures, when checked by other institutions, are decent approximations of legitimacy, which is reason enough to give them a try.

Maxim-izing Deliberation

Cohen enumerates five conditions for authentic deliberation that require some qualification for my use of the theory of deliberative democracy, mostly because the deliberative situation employed here is not an ideal type. Instead, it is instrumental to establishing a better, stronger democracy. With Cohen (1997, 85), I want to say something similar to the claim that laws achieve justification through public argument, but since I ultimately allow in my proposal other nondeliberative branches of government, public argument and reasons cannot be the only things that accomplish the task.

D1

Cohen's first condition (D1) for deliberation is that it must be ongoing, independent, and expected to continue indefinitely (Cohen 1997, 72). This is fundamental in my proposed regime for allowing each generation to change their minds, to alter and abolish their laws, a prerequisite in any republican form of government. Each individual policy decided by a civic jury could never be decisive forever (deliberation would be ongoing), nor could its deliberation be directly steered by or dependent upon outside forces (e.g., money, power, etc.) (deliberation would be independent).[8]

Notice that implicit in the open-endedness of the process is an undermining of the ideal procedure as such. If the ideal procedure privileges deliberation, and no particular deliberation can ever decide anything decisively, then we must see actual deliberation as always in-the-middle-of-things, as always trying to strike a workable solution for the interim; yet actual deliberation must come to a decision—even if temporary. Deliberative laws could be enacted for a fixed period and then sunset, for example. A moratorium on affirmative action for three years put in place by a deliberative body may be just the social experiment the next deliberative jury needs to continue with the never-ending process of authorship of its own laws.

D2

The second condition (D2) is a little stickier. Cohen writes that the members of a deliberative body must share "a commitment to coordinating their activities within institutions that make deliberation possible and according to norms they arrive at through their deliberation. For them, free deliberation among equals is *the* basis of legitimacy" (Cohen 1997, 72, my emphasis). This is a rather stringent (and circular) condition that is made much weaker in the proposal offered here. The norms decided in deliberation cannot be the *only* sources of legitimacy because not every political actor should be expected to conform to the requirements of deliberative decision-making.

Apropos this puzzle, Michelman (1997, 152) attacks deliberative democracy by drawing attention to the tensions inherent in the "liberal" and "deontological" aspects of the ideal deliberative procedure. He correctly places the site of the law's validation in the democratic procedure for the deliberative democrats, but then asks how they can justify a civil government that must always coerce, that must always provide the enabling conditions for a deliberative regime. If we have a procedural account that endorses only procedures "all the way down," the procedures themselves must come about through some process other than deliberation. When deliberative democrats (like Habermas [1996] and Rawls [1996]) use their "co-originality thesis" as a rejoinder to this problematic—that both deliberation and rights to be protected by the state emerge at the same

---

8. This is not to say that participants cannot argue for their personal or group interests; it is only to offer that the deliberation must be rendered independent of organized forces outside the deliberating group.

"conceptual" time—we are left wondering how coherent such a view can be. Deliberative politics cannot be self-legitimating, and cannot be depended upon without other mechanisms already safely in place.

In this context, I cannot address all of Michelman's concerns. To be sure, he is correct in most of what he says if his caricature of deliberative democrats is also correct. But precisely because I think many deliberative democrats would endorse my recommendations here (at least the basic gist of many of them), the implementation of deliberative democracy might be sounder than its theoretic instantiations. For example, "Mark Warren makes the case that deliberative democracy *requires* an authority component because of its functional nature: there are too many decisions for a minipopulus [the formal name for Dahl's recommendation] or policy forum to consider" (deLeon 1997, 120; Warren 1996). Surely, this is another way of addressing Michelman's charge, and making the case I do here, that there must be legitimate exercises of power that do not appeal to or ground themselves in deliberation.

Responding to Michelman's criticisms, deliberative democrats would have to agree that commitment to the institutions that make deliberation possible must prevent deliberators from always coordinating their activities according to the norms achieved through deliberation. Deliberation can also go awry and produce decisions that flout liberal principles by denying a minimal level of equal concern and respect for all citizens. Therefore, I would revise the condition as follows: *The members of the deliberative assembly are aware that they are deciding policy for an entire polity, not just themselves, and that they may still be checked by constitutional principles. (Of course, they are free to try to revise such principles.) For them, free deliberation among equals is a basis of legitimacy in a republic. That said, they still recognize that there is a vast system of checks and balances to which they may be answerable and which attain their own levels of legitimacy through other forms of less popular politics.* Clunky and complex, but so is political life.

D3

Cohen's third prescriptive feature of deliberative democracy (D3) needs to be jettisoned in its entirety. He argues (1997, 72) that ("true") deliberators "do not think that some particular set of preferences, conviction, or ideal is mandatory." This implausible condition might only obtain in some ideal (not my ideal, it should be noted) situation of value-homogeneity. It is entirely possible, and sometimes desirable, that people should actually think the world hinges on a policy decision. Deliberators who have strong convictions should be encouraged, not told that they are not deliberating "properly." Habermas's hope that there will be no losers after political deliberation is thus outlandish. Embedded in Habermas's and Cohen's programs for consensus is a goal (or teleology) of unanimity even though Habermas is, of course, aware that such unanimity may be a "methodological fiction." Only anarchists and totalitarians really think unanimity is a goal worth aiming for.[9] The rest of us realize that there will always be struggles for recognition that go unnoticed, dissensus creeping underneath the presentment of "political mandates." Some groups and individuals will always have an agonistic and contestatory relationship with the state in a complex society. And the hope is that deliberative politics can help give access to more contesting voices so better compromises can be achieved, not so a consensus might be reached. This is the central commitment of agonistic political philosophy—from which this proposal takes inspiration.

D4

D4 is mostly well suited to my use: "Because the members of a democratic association regard deliberative procedures as the source of legitimacy, it is important . . . that the terms of their association not merely be the results of their deliberation, but also be manifest to them as such" (Cohen 1997, 73). As usual, here again we must replace the phrase "the source" with the less demanding "a source."

In Cohen's formulation, D4 also contains a subtle endorsement of nondeliberative mechanisms to serve as the "institutions in which the connections between deliberation and outcomes are evident" (73). If the input of deliberators is not heeded by the representatives in the executive and legislative branches, injunctive appeal to the judiciary would be appropriate to enact deliberative decisions. The outcomes must be enforceable, and that requires coercion.

Finally, making the terms of association manifest simply requires that participants are made aware of the rules. When deliberation is institutionalized in the manner I envision, informing the participants about the terms of their association should be a simple affair.

D5

The last condition is the most metaphysical, but arguably the least controversial. D5 requires that "members recognize one another as having deliberative capacities" (Cohen 1997, 73). This condition does not require full magnanimous

---

9. See Wolff 1970 for a representative view advocating unanimous direct democracy.

"concern" (because people will still want to forward self and group interests—and we should not stop people from doing so as a matter of liberal principle). Nonetheless, it does demand equal "respect," making the assumption that people are not too stupid to rule themselves. Equal respect may be enough to get people to talk to each other respectfully, a necessary condition for deliberation.

Limits

But Cohen provides another facet of his formulation of deliberative procedure that may prove useful in illuminating some of the *limits* of deliberation. He (1997, 73) claims that "there is a need to decide on an agenda, to propose alternative solutions to the problems on the agenda, supporting those solutions with reasons, and to conclude by settling on an alternative." Ironically, in my institutionally realistic model, virtually all of these aspects need to be addressed by nondeliberative mechanisms. *Deciding on an agenda* will largely be in the hands of elites and civil society; *proposing solutions* will take expertise; *providing organized reasons* will be done better by think-tanks than by citizens; and *settling* will always require an aggregating endpoint, and private voting is not deliberative, even if preceded by deliberation.

Even Habermas, the father of proceduralist deliberative democracy, is sensitive to the totalizing nature of Cohen's project. Habermas's main finding against Cohen is that Cohen assumes that society can be steered as a whole by deliberation. Habermas, in contrast, wants to see the deliberative procedure "as the core structure in a separate, constitutionally organized political system, but not as a model for all social institutions (and not even for all government institutions)" (Habermas 1996, 305). This statement runs counter to what most assume to be true of Habermas, that deliberation should penetrate all spheres of life. But Habermas avoids the circularity objection of people like Michelman (as I do here) by acknowledging "that democratic procedure must be embedded in contexts it cannot itself regulate" (305). This book—especially Chapters 3 and 4—tries to provide a checking and balancing that has deliberative politics helping to cure legitimacy deficits while maintaining other branches and powers to provide alternative sources of legitimacy. With this theoretical background in place I can continue the project of arguing for the particular form of reform endorsed here.

3

DEFENDING THE SEPARATION OF POWERS:
THE FAILURES OF THE PROGRESSIVES

My deliberative assemblies must evoke images of Thomas Jefferson's imagined ward system: "'Divide the counties into wards.' Thus Jefferson once summed up his most cherished political idea, which, alas, turned out to be as incomprehensible to posterity as it had been to his contemporaries" (Arendt 1965, 252, citing Jefferson 1984, 1381). Jefferson saw wards, small political debating assemblies, as building blocks for the republic. The ward was a place where each person could educate himself in political matters, a place "where every man is a sharer in the direction of his ward-republic . . . and feels that he is a participator in the government of affairs, not merely at an election one day in the year, but every day" (Mattson 1998, 3–4, citing Jefferson 1984, 1380). Though stressing the educative function of small local forums for deliberation among citizens, Jefferson also invoked a participatory ideal, emphasizing citizen input and activity as central to a functioning large-scale republic: "The absence of such a subdivision of the country constitute[s] a vital threat to the very existence of the republic" (Arendt 1965, 249). But the wards were not conceived as vehicles to be utilized strictly for the power inherent in localism and the mobilization that is more easily facilitated by ward organizing; they were conceived as citizenship-enhancing for the state at large.

Jefferson (1984, 1380, 1399) appealed to his wards to instantiate a truer "gradation of authorities, standing each on the basis of law, holding every one its

delegated share of powers, and constituting truly a system of fundamental balances and checks for the government." Since he acknowledged that some
(even if not all) sovereignty resides within the people, providing the demos a
forum in which they could act as sovereign was fitting to a democracy. Moreover, popular power might be "the only remed[y] against the misuse of
public power. . . . Jefferson, though the secret vote was still unknown at the
time, had at least a foreboding of how dangerous it might be to allow the
people a share in public power without providing them at the same time with
more public space than the ballot box" (Arendt 1965, 253). Jefferson had in
mind what Montesquieu already knew, "that only 'power arrests power,' that
is we must add, without destroying it, without putting impotence in the place
of power" (Arendt 1965, 151, citing Montesquieu 1989, 155–56). Like these
thinkers (without taking a place among them, of course), I wish to *add* to the
separation of powers instead of scaling back and reforming by removing power.
I make an effort here to imagine Jefferson's ward system administered and
integrated into the separation of powers framework; however, my institutional
imagination is checked by an impulse to preserve the basic outlines of the current regime.

Yet, although Jefferson felt that it was critical to "break . . . up 'the many' into
assemblies where everyone could count and be counted upon," he "remained
curiously silent" about the "specific functions" of his "elementary republics"
(Arendt 1965, 254). Surely my proposal offers a flavor of what it might look like
to have "the many" broken up into assemblies with a "gradation of authority,"
taking quite seriously the practice of the separation of powers.

NONREVOLUTIONARY TRANSITION? THINKING
THROUGH ARENDT

I want to emphasize that my elaboration of Jefferson's thought experiment can
be integrated cleanly into our current system, despite Hannah Arendt's (1965,
252) insistence in *On Revolution* that Jefferson's council system is necessarily
revolutionary, citing the wards' anticipation of the *soviets* and *Räte*. Arendt
struggles to read the ward system—and its possibilities for citizenship and revivification of public space—as an entirely new form of government that remained
unrealized even by the American Revolution, at least partly because it was too
revolutionary. For her, even if not for Jefferson, the ward system stakes out a
public space where citizens can discover and practice their civic public freedom.
Such deliberative forums create the possibility for public happiness, a form of

flourishing that seems nostalgic, if only because flourishing seems like Greek to us. Ironically, this nostalgia, for Arendt, is altogether constitutive of the revolutionary spirit.

Thus, she claims that Jefferson knew that his "imagined community" was too revolutionary. She deems it "noteworthy that we find no mention of the ward system in any of Jefferson's formal works, and it may be even more important that the few letters in which he wrote of it with such emphatic insistence all date from the last period of his life" (Arendt 1965, 253). Jefferson, she claims, gives us a hint to the councils' meaning by never spelling out their purpose formally: "This vagueness of purpose, far from being due to a lack of clarity, indicates perhaps more tellingly than any other single aspect of Jefferson's proposal that the afterthought in which he clarified and gave substance to his most cherished recollections from the Revolution in fact concerned a new form of government rather than a mere reform of it or a mere supplement to the existing institutions" (Arendt 1965, 258).

Of course, this chapter (and the one that follows) suggests that the adoption of a popular branch is in a sense a mere reform, a mere supplement to existing institutions, with potential revolutionary effects. Nonetheless, this chapter (and the next) stresses that the proposal can be integrated into the separation of powers framework with small reforms, without a violent and destructive campaign for revolutionary change: "It would be tempting to spin out further the potentialities of the councils, but it certainly is wiser to say with Jefferson, 'Begin them only for a single purpose; they will soon show for what others they are the best instruments'" (Arendt 1965, 283, citing Jefferson 1984, 1380, 1399). I take this same strategy by emphasizing the degree to which a reform in the separation of powers is all that is necessary. What else may follow from such a shift is for a conversation elsewhere and is only secondary; curing legitimacy deficits is a worthwhile primary aim.

Problems of Self-Selection in the Public Sphere

Yet there is more to say about Arendt, because her reading makes clearer how the popular branch is not Jeffersonian, if she reads Jefferson right. First, she praises Jefferson's vision for its aristocratic implications, implications that are easily avoided in my reform plan. Arendt claims (approvingly, I think) that using ward-republics as a form of government "would spell the end of general suffrage as we understand it today; for only those who as *voluntary* members of an 'elementary republic' have demonstrated that they care for more than their private happiness and are concerned about the state of the world would have the right to be heard in the conduct of the business of the republic" (Arendt 1965, 284, emphasis added).

Of course, as I continue to emphasize, participation in *my* "ward-republics," or deliberative assemblies, would not be voluntary, and thus would avoid Arendt's depiction of the form of government as aristocratic. She does not mind self-selection in politics because she cares to "give substance and reality to one of the most important negative liberties we have enjoyed since the end of the ancient world, namely, freedom from politics" (284). In my possible world, freedom and legitimacy take precedence for a few days in a citizen's lifetime over the negative liberty to be free from politics. Let us not forget that Arendt herself always draws our attention to "the paradox that freedom is the fruit of necessity" (54). Nevertheless, she praises the Athenians, who relied on the principle of *ho boulomenos* ("anyone who wishes") in allocation of political service. While they used a lottery system, self-nomination was required. I am satisfied to make freedom the product of mandatory service.[1]

The Party Problem

In Arendt's (1965, 269) rendering of councils that spring up spontaneously during revolutionary episodes, the wards fundamentally "challenge . . . the party system as such, in all its forms, and this conflict [is] emphasized whenever the councils, born of revolution, turn . . . against the party or parties whose sole aim [is] always . . . the revolution." She insists that "it is indeed in the very nature of the party system to replace . . . government of the people by the people" with "government of the people *by an élite sprung from the people*" (281, citing Duverger 1954, 425). Using the Russian Revolution as her proof of "the incompatibility of the . . . councils with the party system," Arendt (1965, 261) never takes seriously the possibility of integration because she is so committed to the councils' revolutionary impulse.

Her reading has its insight, however: if parties cannot control the deliberations or at least the *agenda* of the councils, they are sure to feel disempowered and will try to fight for their dissolution. But formal integration, a separation of powers, might tranquilize the concerns of each locus of power, stabilizing the incompatibility that Arendt diagnoses in the party-council tension. This proposal, then, is also sensitive to the fact that the American regime that we take for granted as one with a separation of powers between branches is just as much a

1. For more on mandatory service, see Chapter 6.

"party democracy."[2] In this vein, Arendt (1965, 272) writes: "If we were to clas-sify contemporary regimes according to the power principle upon which they rest, the distinction between the one-party dictatorships and the multi-party systems would be revealed as much less decisive than the distinction that sep-arates them both from the two-party systems." Though I have no intention of combing the political science literature to substantiate Arendt's claim here, it should remain obvious that if the popular branch becomes institutionalized, political parties can be involved in the popular branch without corrupting it. Perhaps, modern American parties "cannot be regarded as popular organs," and might instead be "the very efficient instruments through which the power of the people is curtailed and controlled" (273). But by forcing them to pander to the thoughtful deliberations of ordinary citizens, the people can reclaim some power without destroying parties, even if they are forced to become more responsive and accountable (poor party!). Arendt claims that the "historical truth of the matter is that the party and council systems are almost coeval" (275). I am trying to make them consistent without a revolution. After all, "a separation of powers, far from causing impotence, generates and stabilizes power" (271).

SOME HISTORICAL ILLUMINATION: PROGRESSION FROM THE PROGRESSIVES?

Jefferson's ward system was not just a thought experiment. It came closest to a reality during the Progressive Era. And the Progressives' failures with their version of "ward-republics" can be instructive precisely because they failed to integrate their voluntary groups in any systematic way into already existing governmental powers. By avoiding the task of finding a coherent way to absorb their councils into preexisting governmental units, their assemblies fell prey to partisan influence, destroying their capacity to help form a popular will. Though they were successful on some educational grounds, they failed to form a new site for political expression because the forums became slaves to politics.

The Progressive Era is known for its "bold political experimentation" (Matt-son 1998, 7), with its major legacy to the modern republic being various insti-tutions of direct democracy like the initiative, the referendum, and the recall. Though the initiative and referendum enjoy widespread use in many states even

2. The term is taken from Manin 1997, 193–235. I do not stay strictly within Manin's cate-gories: The United States clearly has aspects of "Parliamentarianism" and "audience democracy" as well. But his insistence that the two-party system alters the separation of powers is critical in any attempt to integrate a "nonpartisan" branch into the regime.

today, the Progressive Era also saw the flourishing of a different form of now defunct direct democracy. Citizens in the decades before World War I met in town assemblies for public deliberations about pressing issues of the day. These evening meetings were well attended by all classes of the population as well as those of differing political affiliations, and were often organized and funded with public resources.

Zueblin

Charles Zueblin, a notable leader of the movement for deliberative assemblies in the Progressive Era, was self-consciously "search[ing] for institutions where citizens could reengage in politics within the setting of the modern, urban world"; he was decidedly not "harking back to an abstract ideal of ancient citizens" (even if Arendt and I do) (Mattson 1998, 25). Zueblin, with his concurrent involvement in city beautification efforts, was a social engineer engaged in the very Arendtian task of reclaiming public space for politics, but without polis envy. Yet although Zueblin was brought into the deliberative fold by spending time in Jane Addams's social settlement, Hull House, he decided to concentrate on the educative virtues associated with deliberation. Instead of following Addams, who "tried to set up forums where immigrant and working-class citizens debated the issues of the day" (23), Zueblin created forums where adults from all backgrounds could achieve higher levels of education, and with that, a greater capacity to engage in politics. He started university extension programs because he "looked upon the urban college as the leader in democratic political education," and from 1891 to 1908 put most of his energy into this enterprise (25).

Ironically, Zueblin saw university extension as an antidote to the prevalence of professionalism in the nation's schools at the time, which were trying to "embrace . . . the German model of education" (26). Of course, this is ironic only because our nation's extension schools are nothing but forums for professional training. But insofar as they aim to reach a broader clientele and are thus often less "academic," they are partially consistent with Zueblin's vision. Nonetheless, when we consider what university extension took as its inspiration, it is only laughable to see how distant "adult education" is from Zueblin's hopes for it: he wanted to revivify a form of lecture circuit that Ralph Waldo Emerson made famous. Yet "by the 1880s the lyceum lecture system, an important nineteenth-century popular institution that once cultivated middle-class civility, had fully degenerated into commercial entertainment" (26).

If Zueblin really wished to recreate Emerson's effect on the public, it is no surprise that he failed. Though he was also looking to accomplish a feat of class-mixing, contending with lecturers' condescension proved too difficult. Preserving the student-teacher relationship in the context of deliberation proved disastrous, only confirming what I have emphasized here, that taking the educative aspects of deliberation too seriously works against the democratic possibilities for participatory politics. But perhaps even deadlier to Zueblin's enterprise was the fact that his forums became too political: speakers took vigorous stands on issues of the day; since the speakers had an uncontested podium, their authority was not challenged in an even-handed manner. To be sure, university resistance to the project may have been motivated more by fear of upsetting funders than by concern for academic integrity and unpoliticized knowledge. Nonetheless, Zueblin's hopes for participation via education remained unrealized (28–29).

Howe and Johnson

Frederic Howe, a trained political scientist from Johns Hopkins University, also got involved in participatory politics, and with his political training avoided many of Zueblin's mistakes. Howe went "into the trenches" with his political knowledge, getting involved with the famous anticorporate mayor of Cleveland, Tom Johnson. By fighting for Johnson's progressive policies in city government and as a state senator, Howe tried to help reform the political system *from within its very institutions,* moving beyond Zueblin's extrapolitical attempts to establish a new space for politics. Thus, Howe's strategy was to embrace "democratic self-government and decentralization . . . hand in hand" (Mattson 1998, 35). Howe looked to instantiate Jefferson's dream of the ward-republic, rallying behind Tom Johnson's ward, which lived by the following motto: "Vital questions will not be left to the decision of the executive and council alone. They will come directly before the people" (36, citing Johnson 1901, 1).

Of course, the rhetoric of sending vital issues to the people at the ballot box is commonplace even to those who live outside California. And though first established by the Progressives to combat corporate power over the political process, the initiative and referendum have notoriously become just the opposite: campaigns are so costly that only moneyed interests can afford them (Broder 2000). Johnson, however, proved his prescience by making direct democracy less commodified; he would not allow it to be a process of jostling for private votes. Instead, he felt that "heckling is the most valuable form of political education," and thus wanted to make direct democracy partake of heckling (Mattson 1998, 37, citing Johnson 1911b, 82). To this end, he was interested in ways to foster "collective discussion" (Mattson 1998, 39). He gained fame, then, by instituting tent meetings for the electorate to air its concerns. Johnson knew that the lecture hall was not the right forum to ignite public discussion, so created large picnics where urbanites could meet in an agora-esque environment and talk about politics (once they got past taking note of the weather).

But Johnson had an element of condescension in his program as well: "Johnson wrote: 'The chief part of our program in Cleveland was to *educate* the people never to be indifferent'" (38, citing Johnson 1911a, 373). Focusing on education has its disadvantages insofar as it provides a podium for educators to impress uncontested political ideas upon the uneducated. Such a fixation also allows too sharp a separation of the educative aspects of deliberation from will-formation: "Johnson occasionally ignored the democratic public he helped initiate. . . . Worse yet, he tried to block the referendum that eventually defeated him" (Mattson 1998, 39). For Johnson, progressive politics took priority over democratic processes, a sure-fire way to undermine the ideal of popular sovereignty.

Howe, however, knew that keeping the popular forums at the level of civil society, apart from direct action upon the state, would be sure to hinder their ability to be efficacious mechanisms for democracy. He believed firmly in the discursive inspiration that referendums could effect, but was well aware that public opinion needed to be refined for legislation to be liberal, as opposed to just democratic. Such a desire for refining political public opinion led Howe to the People's Institute of New York, founded in 1897. The Institute "became famous for its 'People's Forum' [where] a lecturer spoke typically to about one thousand people, and a question-answer period followed" (41). Initially taking the form of Zueblin's experiment with adult education, the Forum became overtly political, self-consciously taking on legislative issues. After the meetings, those present would vote on resolutions that "were then sent to city council representative. . . . Sometimes politicians directly addressed the People's Forum. Eventually, activists at the People's Institute, including Howe, started up other local forums throughout New York City" (41). Howe's involvement in this enterprise helped focus the forum on political *action*, not merely education or discussion. In the early days of the Forums, they successfully avoided becoming politicized and remained public spaces for citizen participation and action. "Regular citizens were given a chance to hear one another deliberate as public actors and see themselves as equals to intellectuals" (43).

Howe led the People's Institute for approximately three years prior to 1915, when he became the commissioner of immigration. But his contributions provided a legacy: with Howe's leadership, George Coleman founded the Ford Hall

Forum in Boston in 1908, a forum that had Zueblin as a regular speaker (43). Indeed, by 1916, "about one hundred forums" existed in New England alone, with many more sprouting in the West and the South (44).

But Howe was not quite a model leader for the forums, even if he was representative. Or, better, he fell prey to the standard Progressive misuse of the deliberative assembly: "His control could become anti-democratic at times. Although he believed in a democratic public, Howe's role as a political activist occasionally caused him to envision the forum as a *tool* for political reform. . . . At times . . . Howe admired the forum less for its democratic initiative and more for its use-value for reformers" (46).

Howe, like Johnson his mentor, could not integrate his deliberative creation without taking advantage of its potential for manipulation and political partisanship.

Rochester

Among the most famous of deliberative forums were the products of the social center movement established in Rochester, New York. Avoiding partisan leanings by getting the endorsement of the two major parties as well as the Progressive Party, the Rochester social debate clubs provided the greatest hope for class-mixing and political action. Because the social center movement realized that public resources could be cultivated, by 1912 it made its own effort to integrate itself into the public sphere. As tax dollars paid for schools, organizers petitioned to use schools in the evenings for their gatherings, tying the centers directly to public funds, and therewith, to public policy. Topics debated included "direct primaries, 'race relations,' . . . women's suffrage, 'public health as a political issue,' labor union politics, and America's continued foreign policy in the Philippines" (57).[3] Most important, however, "citizens themselves set the agenda" instead of professors or possibly biased organizers (52). And funding was only contingent upon popular participation: "If attendance at a social center during one evening fell below twenty-five people, funds were cut" (53). This condition ensured that the contents of the meeting were not censored with the power of the purse.

But there were two severe problems with the social centers: one was a kink in the philosophy of the clubs and the other was a structural disadvantage. An example of a philosophical problem can be detected in one club's "constitutional preamble":

---

3. Mattson cites original agenda entries from the City of Rochester's records of proceedings.

> Whereas, the world needs men and women, who can think clearly and express their thought well; and whereas, each of us has powers of clear thinking and good expression which need only practice for development; . . . we whose names are hereunto annexed, do form a society whose object shall be the cultivation of the powers of clear thinking and good expression by means of debates, essays, orations, public readings and discussions. (55, citing West 1911, 530)

By making eloquence the main virtue of the clubs, the possibility for the success of the clubs as a site for politics was necessarily curtailed. If the clubs assembled to help members become better public speakers, the clubs were bound to become mere playacting in a theatrical environment, trailers that were only teasers for the real policy discussions going on elsewhere.

The structural problem with the social centers was its voluntary nature. Even though "twenty-five percent of the registration for the clubs during 1910 came from working-class immigrants or 'non-English speaking persons,' as reported in the *Democrat and Chronicle*," the clubs could not help but represent only the particular interests of those that came forward (56). To be sure, the social centers achieved high levels of attendance, but their capacity for representation in any sense (substantial, electoral, or social-scientific) was suspect. Although the clubs were successful at "breaking down the hegemony of America's two-party system" by giving equal time to the Socialists and Prohibitionists, there was never a formal guarantee that any standard of representativeness was being met (57).

The social centers, unsurprisingly, also met a grim fate. Organized religion saw them as anarchic for not having chaperons and used their pull with political elites to bring down the "social" movement. Political elites themselves felt threatened (just as Arendt would have predicted) and pulled funding. Journalists worried that speakers were having an unacceptable sway on those who could not think and speak for themselves. And by the time World War I got under way, the social centers, already in decline, were used to mobilize popular opinion instead of measure it (106).

The Need for Integration

Participatory democracy in the Progressive Era had its attractions: "Before announcing his independent Progressive Party candidacy, Theodore Roosevelt [argued] that the social center should become the 'Senate of the people'" (66). And in the 1920s, "Clarence Perry argued that the major goal of the social centers had been 'the dissolution of class and racial antagonism'" (Mattson 1998, 70). Noticing that in the social centers "the president of the Women's Christian Temperance Union and a Polish washwoman found themselves debating a college professor and a day cleaner" lends credence to the view that at least some of the goals of class-mixing were temporarily fulfilled in this context (Mattson 1998, 70, citing Perry's *Ten Years of Community Center Movement*).

But, in the final analysis, the Progressive attempt to found ward-republics failed for a number of reasons. One that I have emphasized here is that their wards were never systematized and integrated into the separation of powers; they were always a site of mobilization or education, and never contributed systematically to forming and measuring a representative popular will. They were voluntary and not mandatory. These lessons were learned the hard way, but their errors are avoidable.

4

CHECKING AND BALANCING

Let us get back to the business of institutional design. Bernard Manin (1997, 5) traces the roots of popular assemblies very far back indeed, and notes that even "in the so-called 'direct democracies' of the ancient world—Athens, in particular—the popular assembly was not the seat of all power. Certain important functions were performed by other institutions." A standard of competence was required of magistrates, even if most public officials were selected by lottery (14). Notable, and often neglected, is the fact that even the lottery system in Athens was voluntary: anyone could opt out and choose not to serve his polis (16, citing Montesquieu 1989, 10–15). This yielded a populism that had an aristocratic element built in, precisely what Arendt noted about Jefferson's imagined republic.

But perhaps the most important feature of a mixed regime—a regime that embodies populist and oligarchic, democratic and aristocratic tendencies—is exactly its mixed quality. Well-mixed regimes were clearly on the mind of our first institutional designers, the American Founders, who were thinkers with a "slightly comical erudition in political theory" (Arendt 1965, 117). "Aristotle thought that, by synthesizing democratic and oligarchic arrangements, one obtained a better constitution than regimes that were all of a piece. Various combinations of lot, election, and property qualifications allowed just this kind of synthesis" (Manin 1997, 27, citing Aristotle 1984, 1294b11–14, 1300a8-b5).

Aristotle had his own proposals for appropriate mixtures of regimes, ones that are repugnant to our more liberal sensibilities. But Montesquieu, closer to our liberal hearts, continued the tradition of investigating mixed regimes, leaving us satisfied that the mixed regime is not antithetical to the liberal enterprise: it is affirmatively desirable for stability, just like the separation of powers itself. By allowing flexibility and cross-breeding within his typology of regimes, Montesquieu was able to germinate the idea of the separation of powers. And the familiar path from Montesquieu to the Founders need not be retraced. England's constitutional monarchy, to cite the most obvious example, only confirms that progressive democratization does not necessarily mean "power to the people." What it has meant, however, is a rejection of the indivisibility of sovereignty, an appreciation that sovereignty can reside in more than one site of the exercise of political power. It is to oppose Bodin and Hobbes on principle (Manin 1997, 45).[1] Rousseau may also need to be rejected on the same grounds.

Among the various possibilities for a mixed regime is what we have now: "The mixed constitution was defined as a mix of monarchical, aristocratic (or oligarchic), and democratic elements, the combination of which was seen as the cause of its astonishing stability. Leaving aside the monarchical dimension, election, could, by analogy, be termed a mixed institution" (155). As Manin notes, election embodies both a democratic element and an oligarchic one, reminding us that the terms "election" and "elite" have the same etymology (140). Montesquieu (1989, 13) had already insisted that selection by lot is democratic while selection by vote is aristocratic (in contrast to Arendt's typology). Though Manin is rightfully frustrated that Montesquieu does not really provide a good sense of why this is so, he concedes, as we must, that it does not need philosophical explanation when the empirical facts, at least in America's representative system, bear out the aristocratic nature of our modern form of electoral representation. The linguistic facts present their own evidence: "In a number of languages the same adjective denotes a person of distinction and a person who has been chosen [by vote]" (Manin 1997, 140).

My proposal for a popular branch is one obvious corrective to the aristocratic nature of electoral representation. Though Joseph Schumpeter (1942) was undoubtedly onto something when he suggested that the people have no preformed political will prior to political contest,[2] there is no normative reason

1. Manin (1997, 45) argues that "it was in opposition to [mixed government] that Bodin and Hobbes developed the modern theory of indivisible sovereignty."
2. In this context, Riker (1982, 239) argues that populism "depends on the existence of popular will discovered by voting. But, if voting does not reveal a will, if the people speak in meaningless tongues, populism as a concept is rendered quite empty." Of course, providing

to settle for Schumpeterian minimalism. Instead, we can think about how to make use of a lottery system, an idea that the Founders knew about but never took the time to consider seriously (Manin 1997, 80). Endorsing my proposal caters to Madison and the Federalists by keeping in place independent representatives who are trustees of the public, but it also appeases the Antifederalists by separating the power of Congress from a new power vested in an institution designed to represent the people's likeness more directly.[3]

As a prefatory remark, in this context, I discuss only the American case, making the specifics of integration more explicit. In the American system, there is already a relaxing of the three-branch system: the administrative agencies and the media are often known as fourth branches. And California-style democracy is surely less Madisonian than a strict three-branch system would necessitate. So I feel I am on a trodden path. Even apart from the American governmental case, however, I am committed to my institution's portability and think it could find a rightful place in other democratic regimes.[4]

THE LEGISLATIVE ERRORS THAT CALL FOR POPULAR ACTION

There are two main types of communication errors that call for popular input into the separation of powers within a representative democracy. Both surface as gaps between public opinion and those representing its interests (even if we

---

deliberative forums for genuine will-formation and expression would prove populism's very assumption: that people *can*, if given the right conditions, express a will. Riker's mistake is to fixate on voting alone, which need not be the only form of popular political expression.

3. For a summary of the Antifederalist arguments about the need for likeness in representation—"descriptive representation," as Pitkin (1967, 60–91) calls it—see Manin 1997, 109. But this is surely not the place to treat the ever-expanding literature on theories of representation. In some respects my proposal takes a very definite position, and the entire proposal risks being rejected on the basis of its notion of representation alone. Nonetheless, I will have to defer the lengthy defense for another time. In the meantime, the most exciting treatment of representation available can be found in Ponet 2004.

4. I do not bother here, however, with the comparative work that would spell out the details of a popular branch's role in a parliamentary regime or in a direct democratic regime because I do not have any expertise that would make such work valuable. Moreover, I hope that specialists in institutional design projects in international governance or workplace democracy might also see a clean way of integrating the basic structure of a popular branch into those forms of organization, even supposing that the checks and balances would need to be calibrated differently in each case. But the essence remains the same: in addition to the representative structures necessary for organizing large groups of people, the people still need a forum for will-formation where they can be the authors of their laws.

agree that representatives are not agents but trustees of public opinion). In one instance, the people may be mobilized on an issue that representatives refuse to discuss in a meaningful way. An example of such a gap may be the case of health management: since the corporations, HMOs, and insurance companies give so much money to both parties, inaction in legislatures often results despite public outcry for reform in the arena of health policy. In another pathological instance of legislative "error," legislatures find themselves unable to reach a reasonable compromise on an issue. In these cases, legislatures might want to consult the electorate directly, for fear of acting unilaterally, or for fear of being held accountable for a position with which they do not ultimately identify. But often pollsters and pundits are in cahoots, making the gauging of public opinion unreliable, spinning statistics to conform to any result.

Of course, the obvious structural correctives for these gaps are the initiative in the first instance and the referendum in the second. But this proposal rejects the standard model of direct democracy and suggests replacing it with a popular branch, utilizing the idea of a *popular* initiative and a *popular* referendum. Without rehearsing all the details of how each of these measures of direct democracy function, I will briefly explain how each of these functions would be adapted by the popular branch and how the processes would be integrated into our current mixed regime, which could be mixed up a little further.

At this stage I risk being too specific: all of the details in what follows are just suggestions for how to put my proposal into effect and may not take every contingency into account. Yet I refuse to leave the integration of my branch into the separation of powers too vague. Accordingly, let me take two bills through my proposed fourth branch, and then address the role of the executive and the judiciary more directly before I make a brief comment about political parties.

Imagine a possible world where voters were fed up with health insurance companies. Imagine the citizens of this possible world frustrated by the legislature's unwillingness to take action against insurance companies because interested corporate entities fund campaigns. And imagine the further frustration associated with lobbyists' inability to provide incentives or disincentives to the representatives to reform the health insurance system. To whom can the people turn? Let us find a way that they can look in the mirror.

With a fourth branch, organizers in civil society could collect signatures to take action themselves.[5] Political consultants would be hired, and experts would be asked for their input. A bill, call it P1, would be drafted without state intervention. P1 would need to be confined to eight double-spaced pages with one-inch

---

5. See my discussion in Chapter 7 for the details of just how civil society would function in this hypothetical regime with the administrative agency to which I gestured in Chapter 1.

margins, using 12-point Times New Roman font. Signature-collecting firms and volunteers would be enlisted to try to reach the threshold number of signatures required to get the bill before the administrative agency. A major dissemination campaign would get under way. The relevant statewide or national commission detailed in Chapter 1 (CCCA) would then review the signatures collected, as well as review the wording of P1.[6]

At that stage, the commission could kill the bill for procedural infractions committed by those bringing the initiative before the body. Signature falsification, pork-barreling, or other unethical tactics would be a good enough reason to kill a bill, forcing the special interest funding the initiative campaign to start over. Frivolous or dilatory bills could also be stopped by the commission, though only a majority vote by the nine members of the commission would be necessary to put the bill on the agenda of the popular branch. The commission would not have a line-item veto power, and could only vote on whether the bill, as drafted by the groups in civil society, should be given an official docket number and placed on the popular agenda. Any initiative deemed to be a protest measure against a bill floating about in the legislative branch would get top priority on the agenda. If the commission rejects a proto-bill, it must explain its decision with a public document. Summary denials of petitions would be discouraged. The General Printing Office would take care of distribution, as is traditional. And the mass media could pick up the slack.

Once on the agenda, the commission would arrange for hearings, much the way Congress sends bills into committee for evidence gathering. This would help them arrange the days of deliberation. There is more to say about how the commission must go about its task of agenda-setting and framing, but these considerations must be set aside until Chapter 7.

After the bill has been accepted on the popular docket by the commission, citizens could kill a bill only by failing to achieve a three-fifths majority vote at a deliberative assembly or failing to get a two-thirds vote after three attempts. If a measure gets killed by a deliberative assembly, the commission must make sure that no substantially similar measure gets placed on the popular agenda by initiative efforts for three years; this, too, would be a procedural infraction justifying a bill being killed before it gets to the people again.

Should the measure succeed in getting the votes of a two-thirds supermajority of participants at the assembly, however, the bill—now signed by the executors of the deliberative assembly—would then be considered by the relevant legislators

6. In this context, I elaborate upon statewide or nationwide popular activity. City-wide activity could also be integrated, but city government's unicameral structure would require a slightly different, though analogous, set of procedures.

and executives on a priority basis. All relevant legislatures would have to ratify P1 before it arrived on the desk of the executive to be signed into law: only a supermajority of a legislative body could override the informed will of the people established at the deliberative assembly. Essentially, once a bill is passed by the popular branch, each legislative body would vote whether to "override," or veto, it. If any legislative body—the House/Assembly requiring a two-thirds supermajority, or the Senate requiring a three-fifths supermajority (and in either case, at least a simple majority of the other cameral entity)—should veto the bill, it would die.[7] After legislative "endorsement" (i.e., the failure of an override), the executive (the president or governor) would have to sign the bill for P1 to become a law. The executive might choose to veto and would have ten days in which to convince the legislative branch to reconsider. Ten days after an executive veto, the bill would return to the legislature for another tally.

If the executive can get a mere majority of the members of the legislatures (in *both* the House/Assembly and Senate) to approve his veto, the bill would die, and the informed will of the people would be thwarted by their own elected representatives. More likely, however, the mandate of the people would be heeded quickly and efficiently: P1 would be signed, making its way through the (now) "fifth branch," the administrative agencies that are responsible for getting the laws tailored properly (subject to a judicial review of their interpretation of the popular mandate). Of course, the usual amendment and repeal procedures would be available to legislatures down the road, but they would likely be reluctant to exercise their powers against the popular branch. After all, unlike the randomly selected delegates at the popular assembly, legislators are politically accountable and desire reelection. Does that not sound like a well-mixed, well-separated, and well-balanced democracy in action?

Here's another try: Imagine the day when the war on drugs is acknowledged as a failure. Imagine further a day when legislatures make an effort at compromising on the details of decriminalization, but get frustrated at their inability to push an effort to legalize marijuana through the houses, even with the generous campaign contributions of Phillip Morris to Republicans and Democrats alike. The lawmakers from both sides want to stop using endless time on the floor debating the issue, and they think that popular input may be a good way to resolve the matter. Imagine that a two-thirds vote of a House/Assembly, or three-fifths majority of a Senate want to send the marijuana question to a popular referendum. In order to get a bill before the commission in the popular branch, the legislative branch would need the appropriate supermajority of one

---

7. If a bill dies by veto, perhaps the three-year waiting requirement should be waived.

cameral entity[8] and a simple majority of the other agreeing to submit the question to popular adjudication. Once it makes it through one house with the relevant supermajority, it becomes a top priority for the other entity. Two different forms of referendums, statutory questions (like the drug question) and constitutional questions, could make their way onto the popular agenda.[9] Of course, by this hypothetical time in the future, the idea of a national referendum would not so be foreign.

Assume that the bill gets its necessary two-thirds of the House/Assembly, so only a majority of the Senate is needed to acquire a docket number, P2, with the popular commission. By this time, of course, the bill has made its travels through various congressional committees and hearings, including the joint committee, ironing out any differences between the cameral entities. To be sure, the drafters of the statute to be adjudicated by the popular referendum are responsible lawmakers who do this sort of thing for a living. Nonetheless, they, too, are restricted to the eight double-spaced pages. If only all of us could keep our proposals down to eight pages![10]

But when referendums come to the popular branch, the findings of the various committees that related bills have already received are automatically admissible to the commission so that the commission can get a firm history and background on the bill. Though the bill must still be limited to eight pages, the legislature must submit all reports pertaining to the bill, to help the commission do its job. The commission, of course, could also call its own witnesses and conduct its own investigations to pare down the materials for the deliberative assembly, but it could not kill the bill when the mandate comes from the legislature, and it must arrange a deliberative assembly.

The deliberators can always reject P2 after thoughtful discussion. A failure to pass P2 would ensure that the issue could not come before the popular assembly again for three years by way of the legislatures, encouraging the legislators to work toward their own bargaining and compromises with the added advantage

8. Note that the "lower" house requires a higher threshold for its supermajority requirement.
9. Here, I make no mention of mandatory referendums, certain provisions that *must* go to referendum according to state constitutional requirements. To be sure, I would argue to replace even these referendums with popular adjudication in order to counteract the obvious shortcomings of the general referendum procedures. But that is another essay, though one easy to extrapolate from here. Maybe there I could also argue that the Electoral College should be part of the popular branch; in fact, it may very well be consistent with what the Founders imagined. I acknowledge, however, that our contemporary commitment to universal suffrage cuts the other way.
10. Note that Jonathan Swift (1973, 502–9) was able to keep his "Modest Proposal" to eight pages.

of having an informal voice of the people. Nonetheless, if a popular *initiative* brings the issue before the popular branch later, the commission should allow the item to be placed on the agenda again. (Similarly, an item put on the agenda by *initiative* in the first instance may be rehearsed a second time if the item comes from the legislature by way of a popular *referendum*.) But the people's refusal to pass a measure in their deliberations should not preclude the legislature's passing the identical bill in a traditional manner if they so choose, for whatever reason they might want.[11] And so powers are not only separated, but also shared.

After the deliberators vote to pass the referendum measure, the bill would be signed by the commission and go directly to the executive's desk. Should the executive choose to veto, the veto would again need a majority of each house to sustain such action after the executive receives ten days to plead its case. Otherwise, P2 becomes law and stoners all over America can light up after the Food and Drug Administration makes up its necessary regulations to specify just what the law means. The FDA, like the rest of the public, would have access to the transcripts of the deliberative assembly, giving it a chance to instantiate the voice of the people and address any concerns of those who opposed the measure. Again, once the people have spoken, it would certainly be quite strange for representatives to try to veto the outcome, especially in this case where the houses could not arrive at a "right answer" themselves. Mechanisms for amendments and repeals, however, should remain available to legislatures.[12]

THE EXECUTIVE

The next questions that arise pertain to the role of the executive in the activity of the popular branch: would the executive be able to send a bill directly to the popular branch, bypassing the legislatures? Would the executive have the line-item veto like many governors, or should this power be withheld from the executive, as it is from the president?

11. If legislatures try preemptively to nullify an *initiative* campaign, passing a law in the traditional manner that conflicts with a supermajority achieved in the popular branch, the popular law should be upheld, unless it is successfully vetoed by a supermajority of a legislature or the executive authority (and subsequently upheld by a simple majority of legislators). Complicated, right? Maybe I'm being too specific, ignoring easier solutions or harder and more basic problems that I should be addressing. Surely, more work elaborating upon this balancing act will be required; nevertheless, I want to show how this might all look.

12. A final note: Since the popular branch's activities are primarily legislative and because there is a legitimacy associated with its role that an executive generally cannot command, I generally require the legislative branch to concur with an executive veto.

These are legitimate questions, but sticking to tradition seems very much in order. Taking the first question first, the simple answer is no. Executives could offer a bill to go to referendum, but it would need to get through the legislative houses in order to get onto the desk of the commission. On the second, the executive's veto powers should remain consistent with the powers the executive currently has. In statewide popular decisions, the governor would generally have the line-item veto; in national decisions, the president would not have such power. The executive branch's lawmaking powers and oversight responsibilities could remain intact, subject to judicial review if it oversteps the directives of the popular branch. And administrative agencies could make use of the popular branch to settle matters of public opinion, using deliberative assemblies, formally and binding, or informally and nonbinding (though still not voluntary).[13] As a last matter with respect to the executives, it should go without saying that they should retain all emergency powers now associated with those offices, notwithstanding the power and potentially greater legitimacy of popular laws.[14] Though there is no deep reason for this conservative approach, I see no pressing rationale to cause further confusion.

THE JUDICIARY

The courts have occasionally bemoaned their inability to measure the nation's traditions; they need to know them because many individual rights must emerge from these traditions to have constitutional effect under current due process doctrine. In Justice Goldberg's concurring opinion in *Griswold v. Connecticut*,[15] the famous case striking down a Connecticut law prohibiting contraception and the foundational "right to privacy" case, he explains the predicament in which judges find themselves:

> In determining which rights are fundamental, judges are not left at large to decide cases in light of their personal and private notions. Rather, they must look to the "traditions and [collective] conscience of our people" to determine whether a principle is "so rooted [there] . . . as to be ranked as fundamental." The inquiry is whether a right involved "is of such a character that it cannot be denied without

13. This use of deliberative assemblies in the administrative wing of the executive branch has been suggested before (see deLeon 1997).
14. Legislatures, too, should retain their emergency powers.
15. 381 U.S. 479 (1965).

violating those 'fundamental principles of liberty and justice which lie at the base of all our civil and political institutions.'" (citations omitted)

But it is hardly clear that judges are institutionally competent, as our current regime is organized, to make the relevant determinations. Moreover, such traditions, and the nation's perception of them, change over time; this requires a dynamic approach to their interpretation. On point especially is Justice Black's retort to Justice Goldberg: "One may ask how [judges] can avoid considering ['their personal and private notions']," as Goldberg insists they must. Black continues: "Our Court certainly has no machinery with which to take a Gallup Poll. And the scientific miracles of this age have not yet produced a gadget which the Court can use to determine what traditions are rooted in the 'conscience of our people.'" I suggest that the popular branch may be just such a gadget.

There are two places that the popular branch could intersect with the judicial branch. The people could be consulted or challenged. Judges could send matters to the popular branch for a gauging of public opinion, in which case the branch would have only recommending force. Or, judges may be asked to review efforts of direct democracy taken by the popular branch. I shall address each possibility in turn. Yet, since such a large body of literature is already available surrounding the general question of the judicial review of direct democracy, the reader is directed to those debates for treatment of the relevant theoretical issues.[16] Here, I offer only guidelines for approaching the question from a practical standpoint, assuming a more textured direct democracy is already in place, shifting, to be sure, the nature of the debate.

Imagine that day when the judiciary realized it was time to reconsider *Bowers v. Hardwick*.[17] But one of the details standing in the way of that action was the Supreme Court's statement there, invoking *Moore v. East Cleveland,* that the precedent is "deeply rooted in this Nation's . . . tradition."[18] In order to overrule the decision—with the Court's own authority, the nation's traditions—any appellate judge (or a simple majority of those sitting *en banc*) at the state or federal level in a regime with my popular branch could convene the popular branch in an assembly to decide current popular conceptions of national traditions. The judges could keep their questions rather simple, and include all relevant facts and findings in a memorandum to the popular branch's administrative commission, which would still be responsible for organizing the assembly.

16. See generally Eule 1990 for the most famous of these discussions.
17. 478 U.S. 186 (1986).
18. 431 U.S. 494, 503 (1977).

Nonetheless, the majority of the framing would be facilitated by the judicial branch, the famously "least dangerous branch."[19]

The popular deliberation would result in a tally, but there would be no threshold that needs to be reached because in this instance the popular branch operates "consociationally." Judges could appeal to citizen input as a basis for decision-making and investigate transcripts and postdeliberation questionnaires to get a sense of why people decide as they do. Moreover, having demographic breakdowns of voting patterns might help justices do some social science, investigating citizen prejudice with modern statistical methods.

After the vote is in, the judges would, of course, be free to ignore informed popular opinion, especially if the tally proves the issue to be a hotly contested one, with one side achieving only a slim majority. It is also certainly possible that even an informed supermajority might agree with *Bowers* for a number of reasons: as with Justice Burger's concurrence in *Bowers*, national traditions might get conflated with "Judeo-Christian moral and ethical standards."[20] But it is also possible that the popular branch could help settle the dispute about tradition between Justices Kennedy and Scalia in the recent *Lawrence* decision,[21] which finally overruled *Bowers*. And having the people closer to judicial activism and constitutional interpretation surely could have added more legitimacy to assuage the skepticism. In these instances, the courts might still want to overrule the people, constituting their national traditions instead of merely listening to them. They ought to have such a freedom because the popular branch still has at its disposal the legislative capacity to amend the laws, and even the Constitution. Nevertheless, the courts will always interpret those laws and their applicability. This brings us directly into our next discussion regarding the possible judicial review of the actions of the popular branch.

Judicial Review

Alexander Hamilton's perspective on judicial review in *The Federalist* is always a good place to start: "Where the will of the legislature declared in its statutes, stands in opposition to that of the people declared in the Constitution, the judges ought to be governed by the latter rather than the former" (Kramnick

---

19. Compare Bickel 1962 with Kramnick 1987, 437 (A. Hamilton) ("The judiciary, from the nature of its functions, will always be the least dangerous to the political rights of the Constitution; because it will be least in a capacity to annoy or injure them").

20. *Bowers*, 478 U.S., 196 (Burger, C.J., concurring).

21. *Lawrence v. Texas*, No. 02-102, Slip Opinion (Supreme Court of the United States) (June 26, 2003).

1987, 439). While it is certainly a strange move to equate the will of the people directly with the Constitution (see Waldron 1998, chap. 12, and Holmes 1993b, 195–240), judicial review is here to stay. Keeping the legislators in touch with the people and their fundamental rights and values—as articulated in their Constitution—is one of the stronger rationales for judicial review in *The Federalist*.

But, as Julian Eule (1990, 1532) notes: "The enactments that reach the judiciary via the legislative route are those that have successfully passed through an extensive filtering system. This is majoritarianism *plus*. It is the plus that reflects the Framers' unique version of democracy, and it is the plus that warrants judicial caution in substituting its own judgment. Refined, or filtered, majoritarianism captures the virtues of popular sovereignty without being tainted by its vices."

In fact, Eule goes further to say that "judicial review is most essential in the presence of unfiltered majoritarianism" (1584). This approach leads him to recommend heightened scrutiny or a "hard judicial look" (1558) when it comes to the activities of direct democracy, where unfiltered majorities generally have the power to legislate. He argues against "the instinctive appeal of Hugo Black's view that the level of appropriate scrutiny ought to decline as democracy becomes more direct" (1508),[22] insisting that the theory of judicial review must integrate the claims of direct democracy and have heightened jurisdiction above them:

> Just as arguments for judicial restraint based on separation of powers or the sharing of interpretive power fail to carry over to review of ballot measures, those premised on comparative competence make little sense when removed from the legislative context. The superior legislative ability to collect information and to sort it out is routinely invoked by courts deferring to legislative judgment. Whether or not legislators actually do outperform judges at fact-finding, both groups perform with a lot more proficiency than the electorate. If the accuracy of decision-making is to be our criterion, the electorate stands at an obvious disadvantage. It lacks the staff, resources, time, and understanding to compete favorably with either judges or legislators on this count. (Eule 1990, 1538, citations omitted)

Eule is certainly right that mass democracy needs to continue to be checked by the courts, but given the regime I propose, competence and resources, evidenced in capacities for fact-finding and interpretation, are no longer withheld from the

22. Here Eule cites *Reitman v. Mulkey*, 387 U.S. 369 (1967); *James v. Valtierra*, 402 U.S. 137, 141 (1971); and *Hunter v. Erickson*, 393 U.S. 385, 397 (1969) (Black, J., dissenting).

people. Since direct democracy would have a different infrastructure that would allow for filtered and representative majoritarianism at the level of the popular branch, the claims that Eule uses to justify his hard judicial look no longer apply in their strong form. The popular branch is not merely populist; it is republican in its own right. And Article IV of the Constitution requires that "[t]he United States shall guarantee to every State in this Union a Republican Form of Government."[23]

Regardless of whether one ultimately sides with judiciaries giving a "hard" or "soft" look upon the actions of the popular branch, surely they have a right to take *some* look and would have some jurisdiction over its activity. Though here I bracket the question of whether courts should review ballot measures prior to elections,[24] after a law is passed, judges should have some right to check efforts in the popular branch in order to prevent majorities from trampling upon fundamental rights in a way inconsistent with the Constitution.

To this end, we must consider at least four types of activity in the popular branch and their attendant levels of judicial review:

1. Statewide statutory actions taken in the popular branch could obviously be reviewed by state courts on state constitutional grounds. Should the statute raise federal questions, federal courts could accept jurisdiction.

2. A statewide constitutional amendment passed by the popular branch could be reviewed only by federal courts, provided the issue warrants review and raises a federal question. As Eule notes, "The electoral accountability of the state judiciary leaves little hope that state courts will have either the ability or the desire to take a leading role in filtering plebiscitary results. When federal constitutional rights are at risk, the judicial role must be played by an independent judiciary. And the independence demanded must insulate the courts from the people as well as from the legislature" (Eule 1990, 1580, citations omitted). Though there might still be a backlash associated with judges overruling the informed actions of a state (raising difficulties with the practice of federalism), federal judges should retain the right to preserve the federal Constitution.

This far any rational institution designer in the United States would argue: *Citizens Against Rent Control / Coalition for Fair Housing v. City of Berkeley*[25]

---

23. For more on how deliberative democracy and republicanism interact, see generally Leib 2002.

24. For that discussion, see Farrell 1985, 919.

25. 454 U.S. 290, 295 (1981).

notes that "voters may no more violate the Constitution by enacting a ballot measure than a legislative body may do so by enacting legislation." My regime, by injecting the deliberative conditions into popular activity supposedly associated with legislatures, gives popular decisions the force of legislative decisions. Yet it gives them no more legitimacy *for the purposes of judicial review.*

I would go further, however, to include provisions for amending the U.S. Constitution, as well as providing a forum for federal statutory action by the popular branch:

3. A federal statute passed by the popular branch could be reviewed by the federal court system in order to assess its constitutionality. Perhaps the commission might be encouraged to seek counsel if it foresees constitutional difficulty but probably could not use the judiciary because of the prohibition against advisory opinions. Judges could also delimit the scope of the passed bill to keep it within constitutional constraints, giving them a form of line-item veto. In this case, as with others, transcripts and questionnaires from the assemblies that created the laws would help judges perform their interpretive and intentionalist tasks.

4. Only the fourth possibility, an amendment to the Constitution of the United States passed by the popular branch, should give pause to the inhabitants of a country with a California. On the one hand, if Hamilton is right that the "power of the people" should be "superior to both" the judicial and legislative powers, then any amendment passed by the populace must express its will and should take precedence over precedent (Kramnick 1987, 437). For Hamilton, the Constitution is an expression of popular will, which then should be capable of being amended by an act of popular will. Yet, constitutional amendments are quite serious affairs, and it might cause concern that this proposal allows a supermajority of a group of stratified random samples of laymen[26] to enact monumental changes for the entire country, circumventing the elaborate procedures for constitutional amendment enumerated in Article V.

But with further tailoring, the procedures of the constitutional deliberative conventions could have higher, or simply different, supermajority requirements. The threshold for popular "ratification" of their own initiatives could be raised to a three-fourths or four-fifths supermajority, while amendments originating in Congress or state legislatures might only need

26. As aforementioned, in the case of popular consideration of federal questions, many assemblies would be convened all over the country, and some voting aggregation mechanism would be applied.

simple majorities or two-thirds majorities. Perhaps the double majority requirement of Switzerland (a majority of voters of a majority of cantons need to ratify for passage of a referendum there) could be put to use effectively in these cases (Kobach 1994, 98–153). Perhaps petitions for federal constitutional amendments would need the signatures of a higher proportion of the electorate, with stricter geography distribution requirements. Perhaps only the legislative branch could put a federal constitutional question on the popular agenda pursuant to the supermajority requirements already delineated in Article V, and federal constitutional popular initiatives would be rejected *ex ante* by the federal commission organizing the nationwide activities of the popular branch. Perhaps ratification by the popular branch should be *required* after the criteria in Article V are met. Or, perhaps, if the life of the popular branch were on the line and this was the only detail of the system that was unacceptable, the privilege to amend the Constitution could simply be withheld from the popular branch. But if it isn't—and I hope it wouldn't be—judicial textual and structural *interpretation* would be welcome with the help of the public transcripts of the popular constitutional convention, though judges obviously could not rule on the question of constitutionality.

In any case, a court could not review any legislation enacted by the popular branch that had not first passed scrutiny in the other branches. This ensures that referendums and initiatives bear some stamp of approval from politicians, not merely the electorate, leaving the specialized question of judicial review in this context slightly redundant.

BACK TO THE PARTY

After this brief foray into a possible constitutional integration of the popular branch, questions concerning political parties remain and are quite relevant. Though the Constitution itself did not anticipate the formation of the modern party system, parties play a crucial role on the American scene. This, however, is not the appropriate context in which to enter the various debates weighing the advantages and disadvantages of two-party systems and multiparty regimes with proportional representation.[27] Nor would it be appropriate to take a diversion to discuss the sociology of parties or to discuss the oligarchic tendencies of

27. In this regard, see, for example, Mueller 1996, 101–74; Shugart and Carey 1992; and Ackerman 2000. Ponet (2004) argues for PR for the American system.

modern party democracy.[28] Instead, it will suffice to show how the popular branch and the two-party system in the United States could coexist, regardless of the normative assessment one might ultimately make of party democracy.[29] In any case, it is important to remember that the "separation of powers in American states, often producing a divided Executive and Legislature and the need to work with cross-party coalitions, is surely a greater influence on the structure of . . . parties than any provision for direct legislation" (Budge 1996).

Referendums and initiatives (of the now *unpopular* variety) are often said to "contribute . . . greatly to the relative weakness of political parties" (Kobach 1994, 132). Widespread use of *initiative* campaigns surely undermines party control of agenda-setting and works against the parties' general "programmatic function" (Epstein 1967, 261–88). Even intraparty unity is sometimes sacrificed in cases of direct democracy, destabilizing the party system in general. The results of a recent referendum in Switzerland make this point: "51 percent of FDP supporters knowingly went against the recommendations of their party, as did 55 percent of Christian Democrats and 60 percent of Social Democrats" (Kobach 1994, 132). Similarly, evidence in Switzerland suggests that MPs and elites show dissension within parties as well when referendums are put to the public (132).

Ian Budge, an advocate of both direct democracy and parties, identifies four main claims often cited in the literature that attest to the weakening of parties in regimes that rely on direct democracy. Direct democracy weakens parties

1. By removing some legislative matters from the control of the government. In particular, decisions are forced on matters neither raised nor framed by the parties.
2. As a consequence of this, it reduces the coherence and consistency of the policy package that the ruling party is trying to promote.
3. Single-issue groups are more extreme and less compromising than political parties, so popular consultations encourage the taking of extreme positions and reduce the possibility of negotiation and agreement.

28. See, e.g., Michels 1999 and Epstein 1967.
29. This is a practical strategy. Even if parties are "in decline," I would want them to see my reform as consistent with their interests because, at least for the foreseeable future, getting party endorsement is a way to get votes. Moreover, constitutional amendments would be virtually impossible without party support. Nonetheless, arguments could go both ways: a case could be made suggesting that the popular branch would weaken parties and that it would strengthen them. It is not my purpose to weigh these claims here, only to show that parties and the popular branch can be consistent: it is to deny Arendt's claim we explored in Chapter 3.

4. Leaders may take opposing sides in popular consultations, and electors may ignore or even defy the party lead where it is given. (Budge 1996, 120)

Budge rebuts each of these claims, however, noting that they are even "inconsistent among themselves," and are "simply contradicted by other commentators who see electors following a clear party lead when it is consistent with its ideology" (121). Furthermore, elite dissension is common in large party systems in general, and referendums are no more likely to cause rifts than are extreme policies adopted by major parties to help form coalitions in regimes without direct democracy (121). Two-party systems without direct democracy still require party responsiveness to social movements and have parties integrating shifts in popular opinion to stay popular. Moreover, unity could be preserved within parties by avoiding the taking of stances on referendum questions that are not tied to their ideologies, hence actually strengthening the parties and their packages (121, citing Butler and Ranney 1994, 260). And "coherence and consistency are in the eye of the beholder and not particularly evident inside government programs themselves, even where not affected by direct legislation" (Budge 1996, 121).

Nonetheless, Budge acknowledges that "Magleby identifies the greatest defect of direct legislation in U.S. states as bypassing and weakening the political parties, which constitute the best means of clarifying and balancing the political debate. Cronin . . . concurs on this weakness of direct legislation and indeed sees greater party involvement in it as a major way of remedying informational and other weaknesses" (121, citing Cronin 1989, 70, 230, and Magleby 1984, 192–99; cf. Magleby 1994, 254–57).

But parties could have central functions in popular versions of the initiative and referendum and would look to play a role if the popular branch became constitutionally integrated: electors still lack guidance on how to vote, and parties can help fill in the gap by working to fill informational vacuums (Budge 1996, 98). Even if firm stances by parties are unnecessary and avoiding the taking of such stances in certain instances may enhance party integrity, parties could still help the popular branch contextualize a policy question. They could help frame the debate in the mass media and provide information about a potential policy's impact upon some more general policy package that their party is trying to promote.

Of course, these potential contributions only need to be mentioned in the case of a popular initiative. In the case of the popular referendum, where the relevant bill originates in the legislatures, parties would play their traditional role in bill negotiation and compromise. Since initiatives are far less likely than referendums to garner even a simple majority (96), most cases of "direct" legislation that pass scrutiny will still result from party input in the various houses. Hence, even direct democracy as I conceive it here will make use of parties.

In a regime with a popular branch, parties could and probably would still monopolize candidate selection in general elections. Since financial power, votes, and credibility accrue to those who run on large party tickets, candidates will have large incentives to appeal to party resources. To be sure, the hegemony of the two-party system might need reorganization with an institutionalized outlet for single-issue activism, but it remains likely that parties will be clever enough to absorb single-issue advocates into coalitions. Parties (especially minority parties) might also help sponsor popular initiatives because they might assume that bills would have a better chance for passage by the popular branch than in the legislature. Moreover, parties might want a clear mandate from the people, precisely what the popular branch, with its deliberative assemblies, is intended to produce. Moreover, since supermajorities are generally required for popular decision-making,[30] even single-issue advocates would likely want to reach a broad base to get their measure passed and might compromise to appeal to parties themselves, who control large blocs of votes. Also, since single-issue parties could generally get their issue considered only once every three years, third parties forming on the basis of such a limited agenda would necessarily be unstable or temporary, giving the two main parties the impression of relative stability.

Yet, even if none of these informational and framing functions is performed by parties in a regime with a popular branch, the parties will still need to concentrate their efforts upon getting their candidates elected and appointed. Even if they refuse to provide cues and research assistance to facilitate the popular branch's will-formation, parties could continue with politics as usual, especially since normal politics will generally be a time with few measures than can actually garner the required supermajorities in the popular branch.

---

30. Supermajorities might be easier to attain in multiparty systems, where coalition-building is common.

5

CONSIDERING POSSIBLE OBJECTIONS

Designing institutions, wearing the thinking cap of a framer, demands keeping on one's desk near the quill a sense of the present. Reform is about doing better than the status quo without purporting to solve all of the problems associated with current institutions. With that caveat in mind, I proceed to address various sorts of objections that could be made to my popular branch.

"Couldn't deliberative assemblies be corrupted, just like any easily targeted small group of decision-makers?"

As I've mentioned, in an effort to control for corrupted moderators and potential "foremen," federal judges or trained volunteers from the League of Women Voters may serve as checks in each of the smaller groups. But in this enlarged public sphere, all citizens have the potential to be bought off. Since citizens might be susceptible to bribery and propaganda (though these problems plague legislatures at least as badly today), major efforts would have to be made to sequester the juries during the several days of the proceedings. Furthermore, the names of jurors would need to be kept completely confidential before and during the assembly. When serving on a jury, citizens would be prevented from interacting with anyone other than their fellow deliberators. Even if each juror were granted the freedom to associate with his family (a reasonable exception,

I suppose), much effort would need to be taken to keep the jurors' identities away from the mass media and interest groups prior to the event. To be sure, there would be corrupt people on the commission who might, for the right amount of money, compromise the jurors' identities. When the stakes are extraordinarily high, interested parties will be tempted to make extraordinary efforts to influence the deliberations of a popular jury. But such problems plague any attempt at reform. The best we can do is to offer harsh penalties for those who tamper with the political machine and try to overturn results achieved through skewed processes.

It would not be practical to keep high-profile deliberations, such as ones for gay marriage and drug legalization, completely private during the actual course of deliberations; most likely, the whole deliberation would be televised (like some of Fishkin's Deliberative Polls). The population should be entitled to see how their fellow citizens are doing their jobs as citizens and would want to ensure that the moderators running the deliberative sessions are also doing their job impartially. Perhaps all assemblies should be televised, only supposing the electronic blurring of everyone's faces to preserve privacy.[1] While some "value of publicity" obtains in any deliberative situation, the procedure's legitimacy depends on inclusiveness. If we needed to excuse people who are uninterested in publicity, we could not rely on the deliberations, as they would suffer the voluntary response problem that undermines Fishkin's polls, consultation regimes, and town hall meetings.

"But shouldn't citizens have access to the goings-on of all deliberative assemblies and understand how the members of the jury arrive at their decisions? Doesn't the 'value of publicity' demand the transparency of the procedure? Wouldn't excessive secrecy and opacity shroud its legitimacy?"

Navigating between the competing claims of privacy and publicity is particularly difficult in this context.[2] From one perspective, since the deliberative assembly

---

1. While some may think that the only people who would want to follow the proceedings as they are happening are those who want to influence the outcome and those who are treating the whole procedure as a sporting event, I generally think that the claim for simultaneous broadcast here is as strong as it is for Supreme Court oral arguments—an area where I think the motivations are pure and the claim is persuasive.

2. This dilemma illuminates the potential contradictions between deliberation and Gutmann and Thompson's (1996, 95–127) "value of publicity." I thank Ian Shapiro for bringing this contradiction to my attention. I should mention that Thompson does make a case for when "democratic secrecy" is appropriate, though he again runs into a difficult navigation exercise claiming that a secret is justified only if "citizens and their accountable representatives are able to deliberate" to determine if a secret "promotes the democratic discussion" (Thompson 1999, 185). While Thompson addresses an interesting problem, his answers leave much to be desired. Another attempt to treat the problem of secrecy can be found in Manin 1997, 167–68.

is a reform aimed to mobilize the public sphere, the value of publicity and transparency to the public is urgent. Yet citizens are generally entitled to their privacy in our liberal regime. Nonetheless, in this context a case can be made to support the claim that politics ultimately requires sacrificing some privacy for the sake of the popular branch, in the same way that the justice system requires citizens to serve on juries more generally. I do not have a perfect answer to the question of how much publicity is too much, but I am certain that our regime ought to allow some flexibility for compelling state interests, like legitimacy.

As a gesture in the direction of publicity, the transcripts and informational pamphlets of the deliberations would remain public documents. The documents could help judges and future generations make sense of why a body decided as it did, surely another compelling state interest. We might also administer post-deliberation questionnaires to help judges in the rather unattractive process of shuffling through transcripts and getting pointed answers to pointed questions. The questionnaires would also remain anonymous, though we might keep some demographic information available to judges to help them see if demographic variables played a role in voting patterns.

Moreover, although we would need to keep a public record of those who serve on juries, publishable after the assembly, how each member voted should remain private. The final tally would be prominently displayed on the cover page of the final report issued by the commission, but there should be no credible way for jurors to prove that they had voted one way or the other.[3] Also, every statement recorded in the public transcripts would be ascribed anonymously. By retaining anonymity, citizens could feel comfortable sounding stupid occasionally, only embarrassing themselves in front of fourteen codeliberators, the moderator, and the stenographer. Even if the proceedings were televised, voices would need to be blurred along with faces to mask identities. Though I prioritize a true publicity in the public sphere, liberalism demands that we always keep the demands of privacy in mind as well.

"So which is the primary virtue: participation or deliberation? Participatory democrats may feel that random sampling is not participatory enough."

First, from the perspective of practice, participatory democrats ought not complain that the proposed regime is not participatory enough: while on any one question only a stratified random sample can serve as a deliberating body, the popular branch itself is actually comprised by the entire voter-eligible populace.

---

3. The use of voter credibility here is inspired from the work of Ian Ayres (Ayres and Bulow 1998).

Everyone participates—and must participate because the branch's activities are compulsory (see the next chapter for why). Moreover, all participate in the activities of the popular branch's agenda-setting (see Chapter 7 for how).

From a theoretical standpoint, in fact, I prefer to see "participation" rather than "deliberation" as a core value necessary for a republican regime with Pateman (1970) and Barber (1984). While I agree with Fishkin when he elaborates upon "political equality" and "nontyranny" as two of our core values, I (oddly enough) hesitate to endorse his third, "deliberation" (Fishkin 1991, 29–41). Strange as it may seem in this context, I think the need for deliberation arises precisely because mass participation has pathologies that deliberation is well equipped to cure. To repeat the position I took in the Introduction and Chapter 2, deliberation is not a fundamental core value, but rather a way to solve problems.

I would not build deliberation into democratic theory directly, because I think participation is more basic than deliberation in the quest to bring about Michelman's (1997, 147) condition of authorship. For example, one might argue that participation helps establish consent of the governed, a crucial feature of any liberal regime. But when the costs of nonparticipation are so low, deliberation is a tool that can establish legitimacy through nonfictive (that is, nontacit) consent. Here, participation is more fundamental even if it cannot stand alone: deliberation among elite participants is likely to be worthless for democracy without citizen participation.

"Why can only eligible voters take part in assemblies? Why draw the line there? Shouldn't immigration policies be debated by a jury at least open to those directly affected by or interested in the decision?"

Of course, a cosmopolitan could ask why the deliberative juries are limited to citizens. Immigrants may be affected by a popular effort, and my assemblies generally desire that some of the affected parties participate. So how can I exclude noncitizens?

There is no simple answer. Sometimes, arbitrary lines have to be drawn. In this case, however, it is somewhat less than arbitrary. Nation-states often need to make decisions with global repercussions, but to allow for global representation would undermine the extent to which the deliberative assemblies are convened to express the voice of a particular people. To be sure, high-minded largesse is a perspective that should be heard as people deliberate about the future of their country. But the civic voice is supposed to utter the character of one nation and one people, not the peoples of the world.

Of course, deliberative assemblies would be useful in other contexts. Within the workplace, a federation of states, or multinational corporations, this model of deliberative publics could be employed to great global democratic effect.[4] But this proposal concentrates on deliberative publics in American political life because in this instance it achieves not only more democracy, but also textured civic identity. Two for the price of one. More democracy might be a goal in other private or cosmopolitan contexts, but here the addition of the possible achievement of civic identity is a further republican reason for its urgency. If by some chance "world citizenship" comes to have any meaning for the peoples of the world in the future, deliberative assemblies will be useful for decision-making in global policies, for many of the other reasons deliberative publics are desirable in this national context. Within the university, deliberative assemblies with decision-making power might be used to help settle disputes between administrations and graduate students, instead of reliance upon the bargaining mechanisms so often sought. But these kinds of applications are far beyond (and often come shy of) the scope of what I am trying to do here.

"Could a participant in a deliberative assembly who proves persuasive be permitted to run for public office? Could people be allowed to use an assembly in the service of political ambition?"

Though some with political ambition might try to use the assemblies in service of opportunism, I include three mechanisms to work against such use. First, since I avoid the problem of self-selection, no one could find a way to become a juror on a particular policy issue—each one is randomly selected. Because no one is allowed to volunteer for duty on such a jury, someone who wants to use their status as a juror to catapult a career in politics may have to wait around for the opportunity.

Both of the other mechanisms pertain to credibility: those seeking public office could not with ease draw upon their experience at a deliberative assembly to encourage voters to vote for them *because of the effect they had on a particular policy outcome of an assembly.* A potential candidate could not credibly claim to have swayed the results of more than the fourteen deliberators in his or her deliberating chamber, since deliberators debate with only fourteen others over the course of the assembly (though they may be subject to plenary sessions for briefing and the like). Though jurors have access to all of their peers at meals and other recreational events or night activities, most of the arguing

4. James Bohman's (2001) recent work is the most promising application of deliberation and republicanism to cosmopolitanism.

and convincing would take place in the subgroups. Jurors standing on soap boxes delivering speeches at plenary sessions are bound to be regarded as loons. I suspect that during lunches deliberators will want to talk about things other than what they are "forced" to talk about all day.

Also, even if the ambitious wanted to claim that they were able to sway the vote with their powerful arguments, they could find no *credible* way of proving that they were the ones who delivered the decisive arguments. Since the public record would record no names in the transcript, there would be no credible reason to believe anyone claiming to have uttered certain parts of it. To be sure, there are ways around these constraints of credibility: the ambitious could recruit witnesses for their campaign; they could try to tape themselves illegally; they could send themselves registered mail with the arguments they plan to use before the event. But by making it harder, the ambitious would be less likely to use deliberative assemblies for opportunistic purposes.

This discussion raises a prior question: would it be so terrible if a deliberator tries to use his or her role as a public servant to become another sort of public servant in office? I cannot see why I should prohibit it *prima facie*. Since I am not as committed as Fishkin to using deliberative assemblies to turn people into media stars, and since I am more concerned with the privacy of the deliberators, I do not think deliberative assemblies will catapult anyone to national stardom. But if deliberating and taking part in the legislative process inspire some to take a more active role in political life, I see no reason to stop them.

"Isn't there empirical evidence that controverts Fishkin, showing incompetence and inefficiency in actual practices of deliberation?"

Button and Mattson (1999) undertake a survey of seven practices of deliberative democracy over the course of 1997 and reach somewhat disheartening conclusions. Yet, their forcefully unhopeful conclusions about potential practices of deliberative democracy are not completely consistent.

They lament the large degree of deference demonstrated by citizens to experts (Button and Mattson 1999, 610),[5] but applaud the outcome that citizens come away feeling that they want to be a part of deliberative environments more often. Since most of the cases studied by the team were largely organized for what they call deliberation's "educative" function (612), it should not be surprising that the deliberators functioned as spectators instead of actors, and that

---

5. But we must ask if it is such a bad trade-off to defer to experts when the alternative might be deferring to deep pockets.

many came away cynical because their deliberations had no practical effects. The problem of citizen deference to experts is precisely part of the reason that deLeon's PPA could never be enough to instantiate significant deliberative input and part of the reason the Progressive experiments cataloged in Chapter 3 failed. Moreover, Button and Mattson's confirmation of the frustrations associated with spectatorial politics demands a more active sense of political judgment for the citizenry.[6] Their study is very useful for making the argument I do here, that deliberative bodies *should* act on policy not just discuss it, that popular deliberation should enact policy decisions.

Interestingly, the single case study that Button and Mattson label "activist," where there was a gesture suggesting to the citizens that their deliberations would produce policy, was the one structured most *unlike* the civic juries I recommend here. In the case of Portland's energy regulation meeting, there were two hundred deliberators (who were not broken up into smaller groups), too many persons to effect fruitful dialogue. In that "activist" situation, the most "educative" kind of deliberation took place. Not surprisingly, it was considered the least successful of the lot.

Yet Button and Mattson's findings, that many who take part in the deliberative practices want to do it again and get more informed as citizens in general, coheres with Fishkin and Luskin's (1999) findings. The study further substantiates my speculation that such bodies would contribute to the kind of civic virtue communitarians and republicans alike think necessary for the proper functioning of a democracy.[7]

"Why require a two-thirds supermajority to enact a law at the assemblies? Why isn't half enough? Isn't a simple majority all that is required on most versions of majoritarian democracy?"

My attention to detail in this context may seem too technical: at such an early design stage, it may not make sense to impose even more foreign notions upon our form of government, even if the basic idea of the supermajority can be found in the Constitution. Nonetheless, I include it for a particular effect critical in any attempt to institutionalize the assembly: I want to build in an acknowledgment of the sheer power of the institution. If voters get too excited by this possibility for direct democracy, I suspect that they might resort to it to try to

6. For a theoretical treatment of the problems associated with passive political judgment, see Beiner 1983, Arendt 1982, and Arendt 1958.

7. For more on competence and efficiency, see Chapter 6 (on what we can learn about group dynamics from juries).

settle too many complex and charged questions of policy. There may be dangers associated with permitting deliberative assemblies to settle every political question. In a sense, I would like to preserve a dose of "normal politics" and have the population resort to these "revolutionary" assemblies in times of unrest where normal politics seem to have lost contact with the voice of the people, in the case of the legislative errors adumbrated in Chapter 4.[8] But in order to keep "revolutionary" politics at bay, only to be used in special circumstances, I want to make it slightly more difficult to get a law enacted through the use of the procedure. Of course, there will be many that do not want the bar for "revolutionary" politics to be lowered.

To be sure, this hesitancy seems to work against the spirit of what I have been arguing until now. If I am right that a normative conception of popular sovereignty demands that we establish deliberative assemblies as I conceive them, then perhaps I should back away from my supermajority requirement and let the popular branch settle as many questions as the people want them to settle.[9] If I am right that our separation of powers can accommodate deliberative assemblies and that Arendt is wrong to see the ward system as completely revolutionary, why bother with the normal-revolutionary distinction here? As a first rejoinder to the second part of this challenge, here the notion of the revolutionary is reconceptualized: I do not mean to adopt Arendt's (1965) revolutionary category of violence and complete newness. Instead, the revolutionary could take the form of mass mobilization or might be a response to a social movement (to Arendt's horror), resulting in popular legislation.

As an approach to the previous question, I can also invoke again the notion of the mixed regime and insist that popular sovereignty is only part of the locus of legitimacy. Deliberative assemblies cannot be expected to settle all issues (see Chapter 2 for why: in short, there is an infinite regress problem), so some circumscription of appropriate agenda items might be in order. What special circumstances would warrant the use of the assembly consistent with principles of

8. The normal-revolutionary dichotomy was, of course, first introduced by Kuhn ([1970] 1996) and later co-opted for political theory by Ackerman (1991) in his discussion of the "constitutional moments" of American constitutional history. Ackerman never cites Kuhn, but he does title two of his chapters "Normal Politics" and "Higher Lawmaking" (230–94). Since deliberative democracy has come in vogue, some like to think of "moments" as episodes of mass deliberation. I hope my proposal presents a way to induce more mass deliberation, since revolutionary politics seems to have a capacity for legitimation that normal politics does not, at least according to Ackerman (1991). Moreover, in Ackerman's more recent efforts to spell out the mechanics of moments, he has fallen prey to mystification; this mechanism provides much more clear signaling for when "We the People" are in fact speaking and have a voice worth listening to.

9. See Burnheim 1985, arguing that we should do away with all representative electoral politics, and Threlkeld 1998, arguing rather radically that all legislation should be jury-tested.

popular sovereignty? I have no principled answer except to say that we should be wary of its abuse; the supermajority requirement might prevent bad-faith or specious measures from going to trial, so to speak, because the chances of winning popular-ly are not very high. It might prevent very close calls from going to "the people," allowing elected representatives to hammer out a compromise, as their job often requires. Proximally, and for the most part, I leave the Founders' republic pretty much intact.

Our current system is flawed because people (read: "the people") have few places to turn for considered change or reform. The options given to the citizen by the two-party system are quite limited, and political action has become a game of money-allocation by PACs to get access to the decision-makers. Instead of encouraging real revolution, I want to provide an outlet for revolutionary political action. To be sure, there will always be an uphill battle to win a supermajority. But when the time is ripe, it would be more efficient and civic to have citizens decide political questions without having politicians play politics for years before getting a bill passed.

Perhaps as a last empirical note on the subject of supermajorities, I should establish that supermajorities do not keep the bar for revolutionary politics too high. Supermajority requirements may be as silly as unanimity requirements; relying on the need for consensus could undermine the whole political process in a society where majoritarianism seems to be the procedural rule. But the empirical work shows that supermajorities can be achieved, even given the informational vacuum usually associated with mass democracy. Of the sixty-nine statewide measures that went to the "citizen lawmakers" in the elections of 1987 and 1988, twenty-three achieved consensus rates of sixty-five percent and above, one way or the other (Schmidt 1989, 211–14). Also, of the 157 statewide initiatives *passed* by voters from 1970 through 1986, fifty-three achieved the supermajority (287–94).[10] Moreover, "Massachusetts and New Hampshire both required a two-thirds majority of citizens voting in a referendum to ratify their original constitutions. In both cases the initial drafts failed to achieve this majority, but did so subsequently following the inclusion of the Bill of Rights" (Mueller 1996, 180, citing Butler and Ranney 1978, 68–69).[11]

Europe, too, provides grist for the supermajoritarian's mill:

10. Using sixty-five percent as a benchmark here is arbitrary: sixty-five is chosen because it is a round number slightly below the two-thirds supermajority I would recommend, but above a three-fifths majority.

11. In this earlier Butler and Ranney (1978, 2) volume, they offer the justification for preferring "referendums" to "referenda."

The political instability that plagued France in the years following World War II led more than 79 percent of French voters in September 1958 to approve a new constitution. Constitution-like changes to give Algeria its independence and thus end a bloody war were approved by majorities of French voters in excess of 75 and 90 percent in 1961 and 1962, respectively. Eighty-three percent of those voting in a referendum in Ireland in 1972 voted in favor of joining the European Economic Community (EEC). More than 98 percent of voters in Iceland voted in 1944 to separate from Denmark and form a republic. (Mueller 1996, 180)

These are the sorts of facts that encourage Dennis Mueller to set his supermajority requirement for efforts of direct democracy at a three-fourths majority, an even more skewed mandate than I recommend here (182). He argues that majority parties in either multiparty or two-party regimes can too easily take advantage of simple majority requirements in systems with a referendum also built in. Big parties can provide big cues to voters, especially in cases of statute-phrasings that are bewildering in the first place (181). Even if Julian Eule (1990, 1516) is correct that "political parties seldom take a stand on ballot measures [and that] external cues are more difficult to come by [in referendums] than in candidate elections," Mueller (1996, 181) is also right that big parties in certain situations can abuse a simple majority requirement. If a big party can push through a referendum and get it passed, the party can undertake major governmental reorganization to benefit itself for the long term. On behalf of Mueller's case: "On two occasions . . . referendums in Ireland were held to replace Ireland's system of proportional representation with electoral rules favoring a two-party system as in Britain. The referendums were initiated by the Fiana Fail, Ireland's largest political party, in an effort to increase its power. . . . The basic rules by which political outcomes are chosen should have a greater permanence than the outcomes themselves" (181).

   This raises the possibility that different thresholds can be set for different sorts of direct democracy, a suggestion Mueller himself makes, and one that I have made here. But more complex schemes could be arranged: for example, statewide statutory initiatives might require only a simple majority, while constitutional referendums or amendments proposed by initiative might demand a three-fourths majority. Mandatory referendums demanded by state constitutions, since they have already passed through a vast filtrating system of representation, might only require a simple majority. National constitutional amendments would have the highest popular threshold for passage, at three-fourths or four-fifths, as I have already suggested. A chart could be drawn, data could be crunched, and an equation could be calculated. But I just keep the two-thirds here as a simplified guideline before the scientific calculators come out.

A cute little challenge could be posed now: "Once a supermajority requirement is in place, isn't any effect of deliberation essentially undetectable? Even if deliberation produces some changes in popular opinion, are any large enough to make a difference with the supermajority requirement?"

Michael Neblo's (1999) recurring finding that deliberation produces consensus around a middle-of-the-road compromise suggests the opposite of Cass Sunstein's (2000) findings about polarization.[12] Deliberators can learn to compromise and rally around a moderate policy in supermajorities, even if the groups start the deliberation heavily polarized.

The real evidence to answer this question, however, should come from Fishkin's "before and after" findings. In his "selected results" from his eight Deliberative Polls from 1994 to 1997 (a reason for slight suspicion, to be sure), Fishkin (1997, 214–20) reports in nineteen of forty-one issues in which deliberation produced a change of percentage, the change would alter the side accruing a simple majority. Fifteen different issues acquired supermajorities one way or the other after deliberation, while nine of these had "already" achieved a supermajority prior to deliberation. But of these nine, three had supermajorities affirming their opposing side after deliberation! Furthermore, in nine other cases,

---

12. Sunstein's polarization thesis is discussed at length in Chapter 6. An aside: Neblo (1999) presents three cases where he tested whether deliberation produced preference shifts. On the issues of affirmative action and whether gays should be allowed to serve in the military, noticeable changes in the preferences of Neblo's deliberators can be charted. But Neblo labels the third case, of deliberation about effecting a flat tax, an "outlier" because it did not produce the same statistically significant shifts in opinion. Geoffrey Garrett, at Neblo's Yale jobtalk (1999), suggested that the third case is the most important for testing deliberation because it was the one case where all present would be directly affected by the outcome. But given that Neblo's deliberators are always samples drawn from college students, it is not clear that tax code affects them substantively more than affirmative action. Moreover, Neblo's deliberators are not as informed as they are in Fishkin's Polls; Neblo spends less time briefing and more time listening. Therefore, we should expect that lack of knowledge in this instance contributed to a lack of fruitful deliberation. Last, when Neblo (1999) notes that his deliberators did not feel very strongly about the flat tax one way or other, we might use that as evidence (much as we do Steve Forbes's political failures) that the flat tax does not have substantial enough popular support to be an item on the popular agenda in the first place. This last possible retort allows me to ignore Neblo's "outlier" finding because such a subject would not be entitled (by any urging of civil society) to a deliberative jury in the popular branch in the first place because it would have no chance of achieving a supermajority.

on the other hand, issues that had received a supermajority prior to deliberation failed to hold onto their "leads" after deliberation. And five of these cases were ones that had a shift in even the simple majorities after deliberations. Even if Fishkin's data here is selective, it still bears out the claim that deliberation's effect would not leave supermajorities useless or impossible to attain.

6

LEARNING FROM THE JURY ANALOGY

The strategy of making democratic institutions more deliberative often requires looking to institutions already in existence that can serve as points of departure for the institutional imagination. For this reason, deliberative democrats often look to the jury as a proximate example of a deliberative institution in our polity, where the voices of ordinary citizens speak about the laws that govern them. The Supreme Court has determined that the primary function of jury is "to prevent oppression by the Government" with the "commonsense judgment of a group of laymen . . . representative of a cross section of the community."[1] The jury, for Akhil Amar (1997, 162), exists primarily to give power to the people, to ordinary citizens, against the government.[2] Citing Alexis de Tocqueville, Amar (165) finds the jury to be principally a "*political* institution, not a procedural one. It exists to promote democracy for the jurors, not efficient adjudication for the parties."[3] Though this conception is probably overstated,

1. *Apodaca v. Oregon,* 406 U.S. 404, 410 (1972).
2. The Supreme Court thinks it is important too, though it is not as clear about its primary function. See, e.g., *Duncan v. Louisiana,* 391 U.S. 145, 155–56 (1968), and *Williams v. Florida,* 399 U.S. 78 (1970).
3. Tocqueville (1969, 273, 274) claims that "the jury is both the most effective way of establishing the people's rule and the most efficient way of teaching them how to rule."

since both principles are at work in the case law,[4] it does give us a better idea of why neorepublican thinkers often point to the jury as the quintessential democratic institution. Tocqueville (1969, 272) again: "To use a jury . . . seems . . . to introduce an eminently republican element into the government . . . inasmuch as it puts the real control of affairs into the hands of the ruled, or some of them, rather than into those of the rulers." Amar (1997, 167) notes that the Supreme Court is at least beginning to "reaffirm this Tocquevillian vision, analogizing voting and jury service."[5]

Since Cass Sunstein's (1988) and Frank Michelman's (1988) important articles appeared, the republican revival, and deliberative democracy as one of its outgrowths, have been seen to be combating the prevalence of interest group pluralism (Epstein 1988). By turning to the jury, we are able to see how deliberation can be used to emphasize the public-spiritedness associated with a group of citizens coming together to debate about law: "Juries invest each citizen with a sort of magisterial office; they make all men feel that they have duties toward society and that they take a share in its government. By making men pay attention to things other than their own affairs, they combat that individual selfishness which is like a rust in society" (de Tocqueville 1969, 274). For this beneficial effect among others, deliberative democrats look to juries in service of their program of creating better citizens who keep the common good in view. Though surely each individual juror comes to the deliberating table with some prejudices and interests, Jeffrey Abramson (1994, 195) is able to turn this difficulty into an advantage: "To acknowledge that jurors enter the jury room with views and values shaped in part by their creed, race, or gender is not to accuse the jurors of bias in need of silencing. It is to treasure the particularly rich conversations a democratic assembly inspires, precisely because it brings into one communal conversation persons from different subcommunities." Moreover, because individuals are often deciding the fate of others, it may be easier to leave prejudice to one side.[6]

4. Compare *Thiel v. S. Pac. Co.*, 328 U.S. 217, 227 (1946) (Frankfurter, J., dissenting) (claiming that trial by jury exists because "sharing in the administration of justice is a phase of civic responsibility"), cited with approval in *Taylor v. Louisiana*, 419 U.S. 522, 530–31 (1975) with *Williams v. Florida*, 399 U.S. 78 (1970) (arguing that juries are procedural safeguards important for impartiality, for possibility of representation of a cross-section of the community, and deliberation).

5. Amar cites *Edmonson v. Leesville Concrete Co.*, 500 U.S. 614, 625–26 (1991) and *Powers v. Ohio*, 499 U.S. 400, 406–8 (1991). The analogy between voting and jury service is explored by Vikram Amar (1995). One point of disanalogy, which will figure in my discussion later in the chapter, is that voting is wholly voluntary, whereas jury service is compulsory for those without valid excuses.

6. For a persuasive argument that juries are not actually institutions of self-government, but are in fact institutions of other-government, see Primus 1997.

The first knee-jerk reaction—and we'll have occasion in this chapter to pursue some more empirically informed reactions too—to those who glorify juries is that average citizens are incompetent, and that the institution of the jury should actually discourage anyone from trying to model a democratic institution on its basis.[7] Nevertheless, the literature on juries is, on this score, by and large, heartening.[8] "Most civil and criminal jurors manage to take on the role of the 'neutral judge' briefly" (Gastil 2000, 151). Furthermore, "the data from hundreds of studies of jury trials and jury simulations suggest that actual incompetence is a rare phenomenon. Juries do differ sometimes from the way judges would have decided, but it is on grounds other than incompetence" (Hans and Vidmar 1986, 129).

As a public relations matter too, it is clear why deliberative democrats often rest on the laurels of the jury. There is wide "public support for the criminal jury process: 79 percent of those surveyed nationwide rated the right to trial by jury as 'extremely important,' while only 14 percent . . . said that jury trial 'is overrated because juries can so often be swayed by a clever lawyer'" (Gastil 2000, 174, citing Hans 1993, 254–57). The popularity of this institution perceived to embody popular sovereignty always suggests to institutional designers that the more they can tie their proposals to the jury, the broader their support will be.

This chapter is an attempt to investigate the uses of the jury analogy in the design of populist deliberative democratic institutions. Though I cannot do so exhaustively, I hope to show how some designers have relied on the analogy and then discuss some well-developed cautionary notes. I then explore the fact that our society tolerates coercion when it comes to jury duty. Yet the institutional designers utilizing the jury analogy often lose their courage when countenancing

7. For an excellent collection of articles about citizen competence in the more general context of designing participatory democratic institutions, see Elkin and Edward 1999.

8. Obviously, I cannot do any real justice to this subject in this context. The literature is, of course, not univocal. Nonetheless, research does bear out the positive hypothesis and is a cause for cautious optimism on the question of competence. See, e.g., Simon 1980; Hastie, Penrod, and Pennington 1983; Hans and Vidmar 1986; Kassin and Wrightsman 1988; and Guinther 1988. But see Constable 1994: Constable agrees that juries' decisions tend to be unpredictable (so heuristics would not be efficient), reasonable (so we ought not worry about mass psychology yielding wacky decisions), and in the interests of justice (so we should not worry that small groups selected by lottery will be tyrannous). Instead, she attacks the methodology of the studies. She claims that they take for granted a certain theory of law and justice by which they assess jury competence. By assuming that acting in the interests of justice means deciding in a way consonant with what lawyers and judges might consider just under similar circumstances, the social science work already presupposes that rightness and legality precede jury deliberations. She may be right about the presuppositions of the social scientists (hardly a devastating critique in this context), but their findings should be calming in any event.

the possibility of designing *compulsory* deliberative institutions, essentially believing that one cannot force people to deliberate fruitfully. I argue that deliberative democrats should utilize the jury analogy for this salutary feature of the institution of the jury: that service is mandatory and may be coerced. As this book repeatedly emphasizes, I envision mandatory service as a mandatory element of the proposal.

THE ANALOGY (WITH A CAUTIONARY NOTE)

I have argued that there are some good reasons to look to the jury when embarking on the project of designing deliberative democratic institutions. There are many more uses that could be added to the list: Michael Walzer (1983, 309), for example, thinks juries are valuable because they cultivate "natural leaders," helping those naturally inclined to persuasion and politics become who they are.[9] John Gastil (2000, 149) likes the courtroom analogy because he thinks deliberators need to be given some direction with a charge, as jury instructions provide; also, he likes the idea of qualifying experts to testify and cross-examining experts before deliberative panels. James Fishkin (1991, 88) likes the ideal of the cross-sectional lottery system that values randomization and stratification of samples to get a representative body deliberating (even though only the venire, not the actual panel, need embody the ideal in the case of the jury).[10]

9. Notice that in Chapter 5, while attempting to make opportunism less prevalent, I still ultimately embrace the popular branch as an institution where deliberators might learn that they want to serve in public office.

10. In a series of cases, the Supreme Court has articulated the cross-sectional ideal (and its position that it is not required for the actual jury panel, only the pool). See, e.g., *Glasser v. United States,* 315 U.S. 60 (1942) (jury should be representative of the community); *Ballard v. United States,* 329 U.S. 187 (1946) (such representation may not exclude women); *Thiel v. S. Pac. Co.,* 328 U.S. 217 (1946) (cross-section requirement prevents intentional exclusion of wage-earners); *Hernandez v. Texas,* 347 U.S. 475 (1954) (cross-section requirement became of constitutional magnitude, preventing selection of jurors on an ethnic basis); *Williams v. Florida,* 399 U.S. 78 (1970) (number of jurors is not as important as its capacity for obtaining fair cross-section); *Apodaca v. Oregon,* 406 U.S. 404 (1972) (reaffirming the fair cross-section principle, though finding no violation in nonunanimous verdicts as long as everyone gets heard); *Taylor v. Louisiana,* 419 U.S. 522, 538 (1975) (upholding the "fair-cross-section principle" but noting that "defendants are not entitled to a jury of any particular composition . . . ; but the jury wheels, pools of names, panels, or venires from which juries are drawn must not systematically exclude distinctive groups in the community and thereby fail to be reasonably representative thereof") (citations omitted); *Holland v. Illinois,* 493 U.S. 474 (1990) (fair cross-section requirement applies only to the jury pool, not the impaneled jurors on any particular case). Congress too took action to ensure representativeness. See Jury Selection and Service Act of 1968, 28 U.S.C. §§ 1821, 1861–69, 1871 (1994). For a classic investigation into our uncertain commitment to representative panels, see Van Dyke 1977.

Lani Guinier is attracted to the jury because it is a forum where the standard one-person-one-vote regime is relaxed for other decision-procedures that encourage majorities not to ignore minorities (Guinier 1995, 106–9). And I like the division of juridical labor, where jurors have a decision-making function alongside the judge's; this mirrors our general commitment to the separation of powers.

Leaving the positive reasons for using the analogy to one side, I need to establish that the invocation does indeed occur. In this section of the chapter, I show that the interior designers of deliberative democracy make use of aspects of the analogy, even while exposing how their proposals veer from the traditional institution. Before sounding a cautionary bell, I want briefly to investigate how three different populist approaches to making our polity more deliberative have invoked the jury analogy.

James Fishkin's Deliberative Polling

Fishkin (1997; 1991; Fishkin and Luskin 1999) and his Center for Deliberative Polling have created an institution that attempts to instantiate deliberative democracy. It is a form of public opinion poll that gathers an assessment of what an informed body of randomly selected citizens (stratified to be representative) think about various policy proposals, attempting to approximate what "the public [more generally] *would* think, if it had a more adequate chance to think about the questions at issue" (Fiskhin 1991, 1). The informed public opinion has many benefits both upon the participants, who are treated to a weekend of deliberation and empathy with their fellow citizens, and on the polity more generally, giving both citizens and policymakers a sense of what a constituency might decide under deliberative conditions. It is also a way to inject a little "face-to-face" democracy into our impersonal polyarchy (Laslett 1956, 157). Surveys administered both before and after deliberation test the effects of deliberation and usually show differences between uninformed and informed public opinion. Many such differences are attributed to the capacity of face-to-face deliberation to elicit sympathy. Though many different deliberative assemblies have been organized in different localities (including other countries), an example of a recent one should suffice to give more texture to the idea.

A team of researchers (including myself)[11] brought approximately 133 Connecticut residents of the Greater New Haven area to New Haven to participate

11. The other researchers on the team were Cynthia Farrar, James Fishkin, Donald Green, and Robert Luskin. For the writing phase, political psychologist Elizabeth Paluck was brought onto the project. In fact, the participants were recruited through the League of Women Voters,

in a Deliberative Poll on the first weekend in March 2002. The group that attended was a self-selected sample from approximately 500 random people who were invited to attend; we offered the potential participants $200 to come to New Haven for the weekend (and offered another $50 to do some follow-up work). We culled a sample from various regional municipalities to deliberate about two policy issues: a plan for regional tax-sharing and a proposal for the use of the small local airport. The citizens were exposed to balanced informational materials before the weekend of deliberation and three plenary sessions during the weekend itself. The deliberations proper proceeded by breaking the participants into small random groups, each run by a moderator from the League of Women Voters. After the deliberations, we charted changes in preferences. Prior Polls as well as the New Haven Poll bear out the claim that deliberation does indeed change deliberators' preferences (Fishkin 1997), and this Deliberative Poll gave participants a chance to express their opinions to their local lawmakers in follow-up town meetings after the deliberative assembly.

It should immediately be clear how the jury analogy makes its way into the Deliberative Polling technique. The plenary session and the informational materials are evidence; the small-group deliberations are similar to jury deliberations insofar as citizens assess the persuasiveness of the evidence in a forum where the agenda has been set from without. Moreover, it employs the lottery system of selection of participants as the jury venire does, embodying the ideal that each person has a real chance to serve, rendering its recommendations representative (Fishkin 1991, 88). Here, randomization is rather important, and the more statistically representative the assembly can be, the better we can achieve the goal of cross-sectionality, surely one aspiration of the jury.[12] No peremptory challenges skew the process, even if self-selection does.

Although Fishkin is relatively content with using the Deliberative Poll for experimental purposes and to inform lawmakers, he also hints that he would like to see it applied more broadly to promoting popular sovereignty. In his

which ensured that they would not realize that they were to be part of an experiment. The project was funded by the Carnegie, Ford, and Fisher Foundations, and the Community Foundation for Greater New Haven.

12. Perhaps here I should note that there is, of course, a distinction between representativeness and randomness. A random sample (if large enough) will usually be representative, but cross-sectionality could be achieved by other means. Random selection is important in this context because the results achieved this way can more easily be extrapolated to the population as a whole; in the context of an experiment, randomness is especially important. More, the potential balkanizing effects of selecting "representative" samples any other way might counsel against it. I thank Cynthia Farrar for getting me to spell out more clearly the distinction between randomness and representativeness. Irrespective of which is prioritized, self-selection needs to be avoided.

less cautious moments, Fishkin invokes the jury analogy explicitly in his pro-grammatic statement of the proposal. He writes that the "role of [participant in the Deliberative Poll] should be considered analogous to that of a juror. If this event were eventually institutionalized, it should come to be considered an obligation of citizenship" (Fishkin 1991, 9). Tying the Deliberative Poll to cit-izenship is yet another import from the jury analogy, as we tend to conceive of jury service as one of the duties of citizenship.

Of course, there are dramatic differences between the modern jury and the deliberations at the Deliberative Poll. Partially for this reason, Fishkin invokes the Greek version of the institution, where the citizens' juries "had much broader range and discretion than do our modern juries, and they would typically number around five hundred" (87). These ancient jurors, "so far as modern commentators can determine had a virtually free hand in determining what might constitute" illegality, and they had more general jurisdiction over policy matters (88). Even jurors in earlier periods of the Anglo-American tradition had a wider role than mere fact-finding (Gordon 1992; Howe 1939). More dif-ferences could of course be listed: juries have no moderators to make sure every-one gets a chance to speak; juries often demand unanimity as a decision rule and Fishkin's groups are instructed not to reach a consensus or "vote"; jury delib-erations are kept secret; juries deliberate about the fate of others, while Delib-erative Poll participants deliberate about their own fates; most juries (except upon nullification) do not debate policy, as they are primarily fact-finders; etc. I could keep going, but the point here is to demonstrate simply the invocation of the analogy. As we shall see, these differences are rather salutary in combat-ing some of the pathologies of deliberation, which juries no doubt often embody.

Participatory Policy Analysis

As I noted earlier, Robert Dahl (1970, 149–50; 1989, 340) has suggested that each citizen be required to serve on an advisory council to an elected official for a single year. The advisory council would be in constant electronic corre-spondence with one another and would serve as an institutional mechanism to check representatives at the legislative level. Similarly, but with the added feature of face-to-face interaction, Peter deLeon (1997) has proposed that randomly selected citizens who might plausibly be affected by a particular policy be con-scripted to meet expert policymakers and bureaucrats to give their input into administrative matters over the course of a year.[13] He calls this Participatory

13. For a stab at such ideas in the law reviews, see Wright 1992.

Policy Analysis (PPA); consultation and deliberation with some lay citizens is used to contribute to legitimizing the administrative state. DeLeon insists on the "extended tenure of a PPA panel . . . because it allows a panel to gain particular knowledge in the subject area as well as becoming socialized to one another. A longer tenure could help overcome the limitations" associated with the temporary nature of Fishkin's Deliberative Polls (deLeon 1997, 112) (and create some new ones because repeat players would introduce bargaining into the situation, just as a jury that would preside over many cases might be led to vote-trade, a phenomenon we wish to discourage). And the conscription associated with the PPA school already appeals to the coercion of jury service, something Fishkin shies away from because he is fundamentally interested in the experimental phase. But, in PPA, since the conscription is for an entire year, the proposal doesn't quite seem feasible, nor do the PPA theorists justify mandatory service (or even argue for it consistently).

deLeon also becomes explicit about the jury analogy, though he is more careful about delineating differences: "The PPA concept of citizen participation is analogous to that of a jury, a parallel also drawn by Fishkin, when he writes that 'both are meant, in one sense, to be representative of ordinary citizens. Both are premised on the notion that ordinary citizens, when immersed in the relevant materials, can deal with difficult intellectual questions'" (112, citing Fishkin 1991, 9). Nevertheless, deLeon recognizes that "the jury concept is far from an exact parallel. The citizen juries do not, for instance, *determine* policy, like a jury in a criminal trial; rather they are designed to 'advise' the policymakers" (112).[14]

Aside from wide-ranging theoretical design enterprises, Ned Crosby (1995; Crosby, Kelly, and Shaefer 1986) and the Jefferson Center for New Democratic Processes in Minnesota have created a jury institution of their own that is in the spirit of PPA insofar as it is intended to advise administrators. They have proposed and carried out a program of electoral juries of twelve to eighteen people who monitor election campaigns to make public recommendations. They have also experimented with "policy juries" that have grappled with such issues as the ethics of organ transplants (Fishkin 1991, 97) and environmental policy. These juries are charged to come up with "special" verdicts by answering a series of questions, and they are usually instructed to aim for consensus (Gastil 2000, 130). Of course, this all sounds pretty familiar in the context of the jury.

For the Center, the analogy is also explicit: "'Citizens Panels' are modeled after the jury system," and are "built on an analogy with the jury system," aiming to embody the various virtues of juries: representing the public, decision-making

14. Of course criminal juries do not now (other than in nullification) make *policy* decisions in the relevant sense, though they do make decisions about facts based in policy considerations.

requiring little expertise, and impacting upon government (Crosby, Kelly, and Shaefer, 1986). Unlike Fishkin's emphasis on public opinion gathering, Crosby is most interested in putting "the people themselves" in contact with public officials (171). He cites the difference between "empty ritual of participation" and actual policy impact (173), noting that PPA generally remains deficient precisely because "the area where the most work remains is in getting the recommendations adopted by those in power" (177). Fishkin (1991, 106) provides a reason why this might be true: Crosby's "Citizens' Jury employs too small a sample . . . to provide margins of error that would permit a breakdown of the voting to be statistically meaningful." And since the citizen jury is not truly scientifically representative, perhaps its claim to be the voice of the people is extravagant. In any case, in the PPA school, we can clearly see a reliance on the jury analogy.

Panels Affecting Legislation

John Burnheim has called for the end of representative democracy. Instead, he would like to institutionalize deliberation by having small random samples of citizens debate various political issues and set policy for the polity as a whole (Burnheim 1985). With this proposal Burnheim attempts to do away with representative government as we know it and clearly—unlike the majority of deliberative democrats—sees the ills of current electoral regimes as incurable. In a similarly radical fashion, Simon Threlkeld (1998, 5) has called for citizen juries to have the final say in all lawmaking processes. He essentially calls for the abolition of representative government, allowing citizens themselves to say what the law is. At least in Threlkeld's case, he clearly places the whole of his gambit upon the jury analogy as "a group of citizens randomly chosen from the citizenry and convened to make an informed decision" (5). This mode of thinking about deliberative democracy has the jury do the most work, but it skips a step as it allows juries to act as legislators, something older juries probably did but the modern jury is highly discouraged from doing (though it is surely within its power).[15]

Less radically, John Gastil (2000) synthesizes Crosby and Fishkin to find a way to get panels of citizens to have an impact on legislation, leaving representative

15. It is beyond dispute that it is within the jury's *power* to nullify. There is just as certainly controversy about its *authority* and wisdom. As one court put it, "Jury nullification is an unfortunate but unavoidable power." *State v. Ragland*, 519 A.2d 1361, 1372 (N.J. 1986). For the authoritative statement from the Supreme Court, see *United States v. Sparf*, 156 U.S. 51, 102 (1895), holding that "it is the duty of juries in criminal cases to take the law from the court and apply that law to the facts as they find them."

democracy in place. He likes Crosby's idea of putting "the people themselves" in contact with public officials, but makes use of Fishkin's attention to garnering public opinion and having it disseminated to the voters. His "basic recommendation is that voters should have access to the results of representative citizen deliberation on the candidates and issues that appear on their ballots" (139). He too utilizes the technique of random stratified sampling to garner a representative voice. The panels come in various forms: "priority panels" to highlight salient issues to the public that politicians should put on their agenda (139–47); "legislative panels" that use the agenda set by the priority panels to make recommendations about how to settle the policy issue and assess legislative candidates (147–55); "advisory panels" to be used by local governments in deciding how to implement policy (155–58); "candidate-selection panels" to help assess candidates for nonlegislative positions (158–60); and "referenda panels" to recommend to the polity how to vote on ballot measures (160–62). What ties them together is that "the basic structure is the same: each panel would involve drawing random samples of citizens, selecting witnesses, convening deliberative sessions among citizens, and using decision rules to record summary votes and statements of the citizens' views" (162).

The jury analogy in this imagined institutional redesign also surfaces pretty explicitly: Gastil would have panel participants chosen from the jury pool (156). Moreover, he employs jury charges for his panels and desires cross-examination and prosecution for perjury of experts giving false testimony before the panels (144, 149). Nevertheless, he acknowledges that "citizen panels differ from juries in many important respects. Jury discussions are shielded from public view, have a relatively loose structure, and do not use an outside moderator. Each of these features makes it easier for dominant social groups to wield power. Citizen panel deliberations are subject to external review and comment, so they lack the insulation that facilitates unjustified judgments" (169). In the final analysis, Gastil just hopes his panels can embody the virtue of the jury that "all nine justices [in the 1972 cases of *Johnson* and *Apodaca*] extolled[:] an ideal of face-to-face deliberation in which juries [a]re asked to bracket narrow loyalty to their own group and join with others in search of norms whose power lies in the ability to persuade across group lines" (Abramson 1994, 192).

CAUTIONARY TALES OUT OF SCHOOL

Although each of the proposals just described rely upon (and distinguish themselves from) the institution of the jury proper, much recommends against the use of the jury analogy in the design of democratic institutions.[16] Notably, Cass Sunstein and Tali Mendelberg bring empirical social science to bear on the most pressing question: is fruitful deliberation even possible in group settings?[17] Aren't there structural features of small group interaction that will forever recommend against using small group deliberation in the service of inclusive policy?[18] I can only briefly summarize their disturbing findings here and then explain why populist deliberative democrats need not be paralyzed by them. But what these studies draw our attention to is that proposals in service of deliberative democracy at the very least must confront actual deliberation that happens outside the classroom, paying attention to how real-world deliberations are often perverted by forces internal to deliberation itself.

Sunstein

Cass Sunstein provides a reason to resist the whole enterprise of designing deliberative democratic institutions. Essentially, he asks, if there are pathologies to deliberation that are endemic to any deliberative body, why should we want to model democratic legitimacy on an institution whose outcomes are influenced heavily by unavoidable dynamics? In an essay in the *Yale Law Journal* (Sunstein 2000) (published under a different name with fewer footnotes in the *Journal of Political Philosophy*), he is most interested in one of these dynamics: the law of group polarization in conjunction with informational and reputational cascades that bring them about. He finds that "group polarization is among the most robust pattern found in deliberating bodies. . . . Polarization 'is said to occur when an initial tendency of individual group members toward a given direction is enhanced following group discussion'" (85, citing Isenberg 1986, 1141). What is striking about the pattern is that groups tend to "make more extreme decisions than would the typical or average individual in the group" (85).[19] Presumably, what facilitates polarization is cascading and informational

16. See especially Sanders 1997. Gutmann (1999, 229–30) argues that the jury is not a very good example of a democratic institution because it does not use majority-rule as a decision procedure. Though this chapter explores one underutilized use of the jury analogy, forthcoming work will investigate further why consensus or unanimity (or even majority rule) as a decision procedure would be disadvantageous to the program of populist deliberative democrats. My provisional defense of the supermajority requirement can be found in Chapter 5 and note 50 of this chapter.

17. In this regard, see also Stokes 1998, 123.

18. Of course, the point of deliberative democracy is not exactly fairness; democratic politics never guarantees the fairest outcomes. As long as we don't tread into the realm of the unconstitutional, deliberative democrats will often be stuck with the policies that deliberation decides.

19. Of course, Sunstein isn't the first to notice this phenomenon. See generally Moscovici and Zavalloni 1969 and Myers and Lamm 1976.

gaps that do not get filled in, but get more entrenched through the deliberative process: "As the shift [toward polarization] occurs, groups and group
members move and coalesce, not toward the middle of antecedent dispositions, but toward a more extreme position in the direction indicated by those
dispositions. The effect of deliberation is both to decrease variance among
group members, as individual differences diminish, and also to produce con-
vergence on a relatively more extreme point among predeliberation judgments" (85–86). One illustration will do, though Sunstein shows just how
widespread the phenomenon is. In a study of punitive damage awards in jury
deliberations (Schkade et al. 2000), "for any dollar award above zero, the general effect of deliberation was to increase awards above those of the median
voter" (Sunstein 2000, 96).

Sunstein provides a catalog of reasons for polarization. From the problems
of enclaves further entrenching uninformed opinions to the problems of limited
information pools more generally, it is clear that a variety of explanations can be
offered to explain the group dynamic. But we must also ask whether the dynamic
is *intrinsic* to any deliberation, or whether the problem is one for institutional
design and not for the theory of deliberative democracy. Can we control the
setting of deliberation enough to avoid the polarization?

Even Sunstein needs to concede defeat when he looks at the evidence culled
from Fishkin's Deliberative Polls. He acknowledges that "Fishkin's groups do
not polarize, at least not systematically; this result is undoubtedly a product of
the distinctive setting, in which materials are presented on each issue, with corresponding claims of fact and value" (73 n. 6). Other reasons offered for why
Fishkin's groups do not polarize include:

> First, Fishkin's deliberators [do] not vote as a group, and while group
> polarization is observed when no group decision is expected, the
> extent of polarization may well decrease simply because members have
> not been asked to sign onto a group decision as such. Second, Fishkin's
> groups [are] overseen by a moderator; this attempt to ensure a level
> of openness is likely to have altered some of the [polarization]. Third,
> Fishkin's groups [are] highly diverse and enclave deliberation [is]
> impossible. Fourth, Fishkin's studies [present] participants with a set
> of written materials that [attempt] to be balanced and that [contain]
> detailed arguments for both sides. The likely consequence would be to
> move people in different directions from those that would be expected
> by simple group discussion, unaffected by authoritative external
> materials. Indeed, the very effort to produce balance should be expected

to shift large majorities into small ones, pressing both sides closer to 50% representation. (117, citations omitted)

The final upshot about polarization, taking account of the possibilities shown in Fishkin's polls is that "group polarization can be heightened, diminished, or possibly even eliminated by seemingly small alterations in institutional arrangements" (117). This suggests that the pathologies of deliberation may be design problems and not deal-breakers for the deliberative democrats looking to use the jury analogy.

Note how my design takes advantage of these findings: I replicate many of Fishkin's designs like sampling and moderating deliberators; I require a vote, but the aggregation procedure demands one-person-one-vote, so the group decision is not actually limited to the group deliberating; and I require a supermajority to counter the reverse effect of moderation.

Mendelberg

Tali Mendelberg also issues a number of cautionary notes about deliberative institutions. She reminds the designers that real-world "deliberation [is] sometimes inegalitarian, [and] it may also lead to greater conflict" (Mendelberg forthcoming, 5, citing Larmore 1996). Though she appreciates that social dilemma experiments find face-to-face communication to increase cooperation more than anything else,[20] that "talk can create a norm of group-interest in which individuals come to see their own self-interest as consonant with the self-interest of every other member of the group" (7),[21] and that "deliberation among individuals seems to produce empathy to an extent beyond what theorists could have hoped" (8), she still provides reasons to be wary of deliberation.

The jury studies she cites are instructive: "Typically, in a jury of twelve, three members contribute over half of the statements, and over 20% of jurors are virtually silent. Studies of juries find that higher-status jury members (those with more prestigious occupations, more income, more education, etc.) tend to speak more, to offer more suggestions, and to be perceived as more accurate in

20. She cites Bornstein 1992, 597–606; Ostrom 1998; Dawes et al. 1990, 97–110; and Sally 1995 (finding that face-to-face communication raises cooperation by 40 to 45 percentage points).
21. "This norm in turn causes individuals to act with the goal of maximizing the group's interest. Through discussion people change their identity to include the group in their self-concept. The group's interest comes to serve as a heuristic to self-interest" (Mendleberg forthcoming, 7, citing Dawes et al. 1990). Fishkin finds the same dynamic in his groups, though our New Haven Regional Poll is poised to test this phenomenon further.

their judgments" (21, citing Strodtbeck et al. 1957; Hastie, Penrod and Pennington 1983, 92). This will mean that deliberative groups may always suppress the
voices of some because any system that prizes talk will devolve into the "rule by
the articulate" (Epstein 1988) or a "logocracy" (Cohen and Sabel 1997, 330). As
Mendelberg (22, citing Strodtbeck et al. 1957, James 1959, and Mansbridge 1983)
correctly notes, "Class comes with a set of perspectives and interests of its own.
Since the highly educated participate more, their particular class interests and
perspectives are likely to be better represented during discussion."[22]

Since so few of the deliberative institutions proposed in service of deliberation are mere fact-finding missions, we need to heed one of Mendelberg's
particularly disturbing findings: "On matters of *value*, opportunities for deliberation are likely to turn anti-deliberative. And even if they manage to turn argu-
ment-centered, they are unlikely to change minds. Advocates of deliberation
would do well to promote deliberation on issues of fact but to advance alternatives to deliberation on issues of value" (14, my emphasis). Since that is rarely
what deliberative democrats do, and clearly not what I am doing here, we need
to be wary of this intrinsic problem with deliberation.

But with all of Mendelberg's warnings, institutional design still might help:
Mendelberg is clear that the turn to the antideliberative happens only because,
in unstructured environments, it can. With moderators facilitating the diffu-
sion of intense conflict, deliberation still has a chance to change minds and
engender civility and empathy. Even she admits as much: "Encouragingly,
leadership may be a crucial moderating variable of groups' bias against pooling
relevant information during discussion [one of the things that leads to polarization and cascades]. . . . [Experimentally,] groups did best with a directive
leader whose distinctive information was accurate" (38, citing Larson et al.
1998, 482, 493; 1996). It is therefore no surprise that we find Gastil and Fishkin
(and Leib) insisting on moderated deliberation in their institutional designs.
Gastil (2000, 169) notes, "In sum, social status differences in communication
styles and skills are real, but carefully designed group activities can diminish—
or eliminate—their potential to force group conformity to a particular view-
point." This sensitivity is surely a reason for preferring Fishkin's and Gastil's
models to some gestures in PPA that allow the deliberative institutions to do
their work without direction and leadership. But the next section should provide a reason to be more sympathetic to one of the suggestions of the PPA
group, reinforcing my suggestion throughout that service be mandatory. Most
important, though, I hope to have shown that Cohen and Sabel (1997, 327) are

22. It is worth noting, however, that initial verdict preference does not seem to be generally
correlated with race, status, or gender. See Hastie, Penrod, and Pennington 1983, 128–29.

right: "The potential for deliberative failure is no argument against efforts at [deliberative] improvement."

AN UNDERUTILIZED USE OF THE JUROR ANALOGY: MANDATORY SERVICE

There is no dearth of proposals from journalists and academics that aim to compel citizens to shoulder civic responsibilities that might generally be conceived as voluntary programs. To mention but one notable example, Mickey Kaus has urged mandatory conscription in the United States as well as compulsory national community service for young Americans (Kaus 1992, 78–102). In service of a "civic liberal" agenda, he aims for equalization of social standing through the race-mixing and class-mixing that such programs should bring about. Believing that equality will remain elusive in America until we end the obsession of the "money liberals" with equality of resources, he proposes several compulsory programs targeted to level social standing.[23]

Though proposals for new compulsory programs are generally viewed with suspicion by the citizenry (how many have been adopted in your lifetime?), the jury is one old institution that enjoys wide participation and continued support despite its mandatory character.[24] In our voluntarist public sphere where political participation is generally optional, juries embody the lowest form of freedom of choice (Walzer 1983, 163). And there is little momentum afoot to do away with the jury system altogether; even its most trenchant critics do not impugn its mandatory character.[25] It is therefore surprising to see so few deliberative democrats who otherwise make use of the jury analogy argue for mandatory regimes. Gastil (2000, 141), for example, writes: "Some might take the jury example a step farther and compel participation on panels, but I prefer permitting citizens to make their own choices." There are some very good reasons to compel citizens to do so from the perspective of civic responsibility and legitimacy, as well as representativeness and impartiality, all

---

23. The centrality of the equality of social standing was promulgated most saliently by Shklar (1991).

24. For the proposition that "by the end of their service, the vast majority of jurors, even those who never serve in trials, have favorable attitudes toward jury service and confidence in the jury system," see Diamond 1993, 285, citing Munsterman et al. 1991, app. C (1991) (finding 72 to 90 percent of jurors having a positive attitude toward jury service after serving and finding improvement in the attitudes of 58 to 86 percent of their 8,468 respondents). See also Pabst 1976 (finding two-thirds of jurors becoming more favorable or staying favorable after service).

25. With shorter terms, there is even less unwillingness to serve (Pabst 1977).

considerations militating toward mandatory jury duty and mandatory participation in deliberative assemblies.

Civic Responsibility and Legitimacy

Courts have often perceived jury service as part of a citizen's responsibility to
his or her polity. In *Taylor v. Louisiana,* the Court affirmed that trial by jury
exists because "sharing in the administration of justice is a phase of civic responsibility."[26] Also, in *United States v. Raszkiewicz,* the Seventh Circuit noted that
part of jury service is "furthering the notion that participation in the administration of justice is a part of one's civic responsibility."[27] This general principle,
that jury service is bound up with civic responsibility, is clearly part of the reason for mandatory service laws. To be sure, not uncommonly, people try to get
excused. But as a society we think of jury service as one of the few duties of citizenship. As Abramson (1994, 252) writes, "Jury duty falls upon millions of
Americans each year, making the jury system the most widespread example of
participatory democracy in the United States today, despite all the loopholes
that permit persons to escape service." In 1990, for example, 400,000 citizens
showed up in federal district courts for voir dire; many more were utilized in
the state courts (252).

Deliberative democrats are also sensitive to the role of civic participation in
the healthy functioning of a republican polity, especially when they emphasize—as I do—participation over deliberation.[28] (Remember that Tocqueville
thought of the jury as the republican institution *par excellence.*) To the extent
that popular sovereignty is an ideal of the deliberative democrats—even if they
don't go as far as Amar (1998, 119–33; 1994) does in making it wholly central
to the American scheme of government—achieving it in a "nonfictively attributable sense" (Michelman 1997, 146–47) must be part of the project of institutional redesign in service of making outcomes more deliberative, hence more
legitimately emerging from the voice of the people. By trying to crystallize
popular will-formation with their technocratic tools, deliberative democrats
recommend the expansion of popular sovereignty and usually believe that legitimation is tied up with subjects living under laws they themselves authored. As
Habermas (1996, 110), one of the fathers of deliberative democracy, insists,
"Deliberative politics acquires its legitimating force from the discursive structure

26. 419 U.S. 522, 530–31 (1975) (citing *Thiel v. S. Pac. Co.,* 328 U.S. 217, 227 [1946]) (Frankfurter, J., dissenting).
27. 169 F.3d 459, 466 (7th Cir. 1999).
28. See my argument for this preference in Chapter 5.

of . . . will-formation" (304). Thus, designers trying to tailor a discursive or deliberative structure no doubt pay attention to the legitimation their institutions can help bring about.

At the least, we can say that though most of the institutional designers I have just discussed generally leave our three-branch representative regime untouched by the *direct* influence of popular deliberation,[29] they all imagine their institutions as garnering the voice of the people more deliberately and deliberatively than electoral politics, thereby contributing to popular sovereignty. And with popular sovereignty, they are able to achieve the project of authorship, or at least approximate it better (though all come shy of what I argue would be the appropriate level of popular sovereignty. Although many deliberative democrats surely favor citizen participation for its "educative" effects,[30] effects Tocqueville (1969, 273, 275) praised the jury for, participation is also prized (by my proposal especially) for its capacity to fulfill Habermas's ideal of the legitimation of truly deliberative politics, a politics of popular sovereignty. Fishkin (1997, 40), deLeon (1997, 87–91, 94, 103, 106, 110, 115), Gastil (2000, 22–23), and I all cite Habermas in the course of making our arguments for why popular deliberation should be institutionalized.[31] Crosby (Crosby, Kelly, and Schaefer 1986, 171) also defines his projects in terms of getting "the people themselves" to influence policy, a clear appeal to popular sovereignty.

Though no one imagines that all can participate in the free and equal conversations that deliberative democrats prize, neither does anyone imagine that representative government as we have it satisfies the aspiration for the practice of deliberative democracy.[32] To be sure, the argument of this book is that some

---

29. Threlkeld and Burnheim are notable, but underdeveloped, naïve, and utopian (in Burheim's case self-consciously so), exceptions.

30. See, e.g., Dewey 1954, 208–9, 211, 218. Carole Pateman (1970, 42) also values participation for its "educative" function, "educative in the very widest sense, including both the psychological aspect and the gaining practice in democratic skills and procedures." Fishkin (1991, 52) notes that "this argument works best in small-scale, face-to-face settings, particularly democracy in the workplace and in aspects of the local political environment that are close to home." This helps explain why I have focused only upon the deliberative democrats with "polis envy," and have not looked in detail at the glut of proposals for teledemocracy, making use of telecommunications and internet technology. For these, see, e.g., Becker 1981 and Etzioni 1972.

31. As should become clear, I do not think it accidental that deLeon makes the most elaborate use of Habermas, as his is the program most likely to require mandatory service.

32. It is only the populist strain that concerns me here. Many institutional designers are content to try to make our existing governmental bodies, such as Congress and the Supreme Court, more deliberative, but those approaches are not the focus of this chapter (or this book—see Chapter 2 again for why). Rawls (1996) and Ferejohn (2000) both focus their energies on making currently existing institutions more deliberative and fail to exercise more complete institutional imagination (and fail to trust the populace).

go too far in trying to incite revolution and that most do not go far enough in getting the populace to participate. Generally, the programs investigated here do indeed look to ordinary citizens—just as the jury does—to express their informed preferences. Abramson (1994, 11), invoking Aristotle and the jury, agrees too: "Aristotle suggested that democracy's chief virtue was the way it permitted ordinary persons drawn from different walks of life to achieve a 'collective wisdom' that none could achieve alone. At its best, the jury is the last, best refuge of this connection among democracy, deliberation, and the achievement of wisdom by ordinary persons." The populist deliberative democrats envision yet another nexus for Aristotle's "Doctrine of the Wisdom of the Multitude," as Jeremy Waldron (1999, 94) has called it.[33] But it can only serve as this site if citizens must meet and greet each other there,[34] if our republican democracy allows us to compel service, to compel a few days of self-sacrifice.[35]

Of course, the standard line in our Madisonian regime is that republican politics must be satisfied by—indeed it positively requires—representative politics. Popular sovereignty as a condition for legitimacy is met by electoral politics for most content with the status quo. In the most authoritative statement by Madison, a republic is in fact defined as "a government in which the scheme of representation takes place" (Kramnick 1987, 126). Republicans have always trusted representatives for their capacity to deliberate, showing a certain sensitivity or anticipation of deliberative democracy in republicanism: James Madison wanted "to refine and enlarge the public views by passing them through the medium of a chosen body of citizens" (126). And Alexander Hamilton saw the representative body as an "opportunity for cool and sedate reflection" (410).

I, however, contend that the ongoing social project of authorship—the proffered definition of popular self-government—demands more vigorous citizen participation.[36] The populist deliberative democrats like myself also generally care about representation (as we shall see), but I am more insistent that citizens have power against potential governmental oppression. This is, of course, one of the primary reasons for the institution of the jury as announced in *Apodaca*,[37]

33. For another famous version of this argument, see Rawls 1971, 358–59 ("Discussion is a way of combining information and enlarging the range of arguments. At least in the course of time, the effects of common deliberation seem bound to improve matters").

34. Waldron thinks that the wisdom of the multitude is only in effect when a body meets together in an assembly and the members greet each other face-to-face (Waldron 1999, 115, citing Aristotle 1984, 1281b1).

35. For the theory that republicanism demands the virtue of self-sacrifice, see generally Montesquieu 1989 and Amar 1994, 759.

36. For the longer and more romantic version of this argument, see Barber 1984.

37. *Apodaca v. Oregon*, 406 U.S. 404, 410 (1972).

and partially because of this function, we put it upon each ordinary citizen to partake; even those who have no articulated interest in self-government are recruited for jury service. The pool we draw from is "representative" too, just as republicanism would prefer. But this pool is of ordinary folks with no property, gender, or racial prerequisites (anymore), as popular sovereignty would prefer.

In the case of the popular branch, the argument should be even stronger for mandatory service than it is in the jury: Richard Primus is right that juries are better thought of as institutions of "other-government," where ordinary citizens rule over others (Primus 1997); by contrast, the popular branch, especially if heeded by the government in a more responsive form than they are in the experimental and theoretical instantiations, is much more obviously a potential exercise of self-government. We regularly coerce citizens to get a civics education in grade school, so its educative function (even if not its primary use) can be compelled. Moreover, we do not allow people to opt out of the jury system because they are happy to let justice be done without their direct input; we simply believe justice *cannot* be done without their input. So too, popular deliberation, to achieve fully legitimate and democratic results, must include even those who claim to have no interest in participating. Leaving it to citizens to decide whether their policy preferences are to be part of the civic voice is wholly irresponsible,[38] especially if populist deliberative democrats really care, as they say they do (Cohen and Sabel 1997, 327), about an inclusive civic voice articulated directly from free and equals. As one court has noted, "Jurors may be citizen soldiers, but they are soldiers nonetheless, and like soldiers of any sort, they may be asked to perform distasteful duties. Their participation in publicized trials may force them into the limelight against their wishes."[39] Similarly, we should not cringe at the idea that popular sovereignty might demand something of citizens that they otherwise might not wish to do.[40]

---

38. For more on the importance of the civic voice, see Sandel 1996. I guess it would be irresponsible to unload this rhetoric without acknowledging that our current proxy for civic voice, voting, obviously does not compel participation, despite its direct contribution to what we have of popular sovereignty. Frankly, I can make no sense of our indulgent voluntarism there, though I'm fairly cynical about why that regime is in place: it is no secret that voters are whiter, richer, and better educated than nonvoters and mandating voting might garner a more inclusive civic voice, something to which I'm not always sure the elected class is wholly committed. In any case, conveniently for my argument here, we do compel jury service, a far more time-consuming and intensive civic responsibility.

39. In re *Globe Newspaper Co.,* 920 F.2d 88, 98 (1st Cir. 1990).

40. This raises the further issue of whether deliberative assemblies that decide policy should be kept secret, since that is the context of the court's proclamation. There is another feature of institutional design that might help guard against self-interested behavior in the context of popular deliberative democracy: publicity. Though jury deliberations are generally protected by a

DeLeon is right, however, to invoke John Dryzek as a caution against excessive glorification of participation as such: "Participatory democracy itself has an
ambiguous potential." Without true deliberation, "it will only add to the bur-
dens of complexity. On the other hand, [deliberation] without open participation will remain hobbled by the vestiges of control by a privileged group" of
agenda-setters and legislators (deLeon 1887, 94, citing Dryzek 1990, 72). Thus,
populist deliberative democrats must compel service in their well-designed
institutions, not merely because participation itself contributes to legitimacy
and not merely because civic duties make for hearty citizens. Rather, the institutions must use the feature of compulsion to help forward the agenda of fruitful deliberation. Fruitful deliberation can only happen if deliberative assemblies
are representative and impartial, which they cannot be unless all citizens are
equally likely to serve in them.

Representativeness and Impartiality

Surely part of the reason that the jury system compels service is that there is
both a constitutional and statutory requirement that justice be delivered locally,
by a representative body of peers. The venue provision in Article III requires
all criminal trials to be within the state in which the crime was committed, and
the Sixth Amendment requires criminal trials "by an impartial jury of the
State and district wherein the crime shall have been committed."[41] Statutorily,

---

regime of secrecy, the deliberative democratic institutions discussed here tend to glorify the
virtues of giving the media access to the panels. There is good reason to believe that this might
help in the quest for public-spiritedness in deliberation. Mendelberg explains:

> A . . . favorable answer comes from experimental research by Tetlock, and Kruglanski and
> Freund. These studies found that when people are told in advance that their judgments will
> become public, they are more likely to treat evidence objectively, and less likely to allow their
> reasoning to be biased. The mere anticipation of public deliberation may serve the function
> of democratic education. Accountability, believes Tetlock, as do the deliberative theorists
> Gutmann and Thompson, is at the heart of the matter. If people know that they will be held
> accountable for their judgments, they will expend more cognitive effort and give priority to
> the goal of accuracy rather than the goal of buttressing their prior beliefs.

Mendelberg (forthcoming, 33, citing Gutmann and Thompson 1996; Kruglanski and Freund
1983; Tetlock 1983 and 1985; and Tetlock and Kim 1987). But see Kuran 1995 (arguing that though
publicity might work in favor of seemingly more progressive outcomes, it also provides incentives
to lie). This, of course, raises yet another interesting moment of comparison in the use of the
juror analogy in the design of deliberative democratic institutions. I hope to take up this question at a later date, but offer a compromise in Chapter 5.
    41. U.S. Const., Art. III, § 2, cl. 3; U.S. Const., Amend. VI. For a discussion of the require-
ments, see Alexander 1991.

Congress has enacted the Jury Selection and Service Act of 1968.[42] It provides for a jury "selected at random from a fair cross section of the community,"[43] and requires that voter lists be supplemented when necessary, essentially recognizing that nonwhites, the poor, the uneducated, and young register to vote at much lower rates than others.[44] Embedded in the various efforts to ensure that the cross-sectional requirement is met is a commitment to recruiting members of the community who might not otherwise volunteer. We do this at least in part because the representative aspect of the jury (or at least of the venire, the pool from which the smaller, or petit, jury is selected) contributes to our conception of the jury's fairness and impartiality.[45] Without a variety of perspectives in the deliberation chamber, we have the sense that we may be skewing the conversation in the jury room.[46]

Similarly, most designers of deliberative democratic institutions are rather sensitive to the issues of representation and impartiality. Most wish to stress, with Abramson (1994, 8), that there are "two understandings of the jury's role in a democracy. The first envisions the jury as essentially a representative body, where jurors act as spokespersons for competing group interests. Such a view comfortably fits the jury to prevailing models of interest group behavior; it assumes that jurors inevitably favor their own kind and vote according to narrow group loyalties." The other understanding, the one most deliberative democrats prefer (though the more realistic models, like my own, understand that interest-group pluralism has its place), is conceiving of the jury as the site of rational discourse, where interest-free deliberation takes place, where impartiality leads the way to justice. Of course, this latter model is highly idealized, and cases of self-government, as opposed to other-government, will be much more likely to trigger self-interested behavior during deliberations. Therefore, deliberative democrats who aspire for a more participatory politics must pay very careful attention, not only to the structure of deliberation, but also to the difficult question of just who gets to participate in the deliberative forums.

Generally speaking, though representativeness is very high priority for Fishkin, PPA, and Gastil, most of the programs for instituting deliberative democracy

42. 28 U.S.C. §§ 1821, 1861–69, 1871 (1994).
43. 28 U.S.C. § 1861.
44. 28 U.S.C. § 1863 (b) (2); Van Dyke 1977, 88–93. For the standard work on voter turnout and the correlation between race, class, and participation, see Rosenstone and Hansen 1993, Verba et al. 1993, and Lijphart 1997.
45. See generally *Irvin v. Dowd,* 366 U.S. 717 (1961); *Taylor v. Louisiana,* 419 U.S. 522 (1975); and *Carter v. Jury Comm.,* 396 U.S. 333 (1970).
46. Of course, the Equal Protection Clause prevents excluding certain groups from the jury as well.

considered here tend to rely on voluntary service.[47] Nevertheless, they all employ the tools of random sampling to claim for their institutions credibility on the basis of scientific representativeness. Utilizing the fair cross-section principle associated with the jury,[48] they each recognize that the success of "selling" their institution and its results to the public relies on its claim to be representative of the community at large. Without the representative quality, the civic voice that the programs garner fails the test of legitimacy—it is not authored in a nonfictively attributable sense (Michelman 1997, 146–47). Therefore, they each devote considerable energy to enunciating how their proposal lives up to this ideal. Obviously, I think mine does better on this score.

Fishkin (1997; 64–96; 1999b, 279–90) is most interested in challenging the standard measures of public opinion as the voice of the people. Instead, he likes to gather at his Polls a truly stratified random (so representative) sample, paying attention to common ways of classifying individuals, including policy preference, race, ethnicity, age, and the like. Utilizing this method, he is able to claim that his proposal is consistent with representative democracy, and is not a pure form of direct or plebiscitary democracy (Fishkin 1991, 16–17, 22–25, 33, 35, 38, 42–46, 50–51, 59, 67, 77, 81, 92, 99, 100). By technocratically imposing a scheme of representation that coheres with an underlying ideal of fairness, he is able to emphasize a feature of the jury system that even the jury system often fails to achieve: a fair cross-section of the community. Since his Polls can accommodate approximately five hundred participants, possibilities for more complete representation emerge. Nevertheless, even in his utopian moments, he fails to imagine a society compelled to deliberate as the jury system contemplates (though he gestures in that direction on one occasion). Perhaps the excuse is that we can force people to show up but not to talk; better that we should at least find people who want to do both.

The PPA models generally aim for representativeness too, though Crosby's (Crosby, Kelly, and Schaefer 1986, 170, 171, 174, 175) policy juries are so small (as small as regular juries!) that their aspiration for representativeness must always remain aspirational at best. Nevertheless, he is keenly aware of the ideal: he notes that "lack of representativeness of the participants is a real shortcoming," and he devotes substantial attention to "participant selection" in service of legitimating the deliberation of his policy juries. Although his desire for representativeness is

47. Since many of the designers attempt to implement their proposals experimentally, insisting upon compulsory service makes little sense. But the reason I focus upon it here is that the vast majority of deliberative democrats do not even aspire to mandate deliberative institutions even though they take their inspiration from the jury.

48. See the cases cited in note 10.

most forcefully urged because of the potential for manipulation by special interests (175), his commitment is unwavering; his team makes an effort to include in
deliberative bodies primarily attitudinal representation as opposed to more typical demographic representation, which is clearly impossible to accomplish
with his small juries. Precisely because he is sensitive to the perception of bias
in choosing participants, he aims for a greater legitimacy by doing as good a
job as possible at getting a fair cross-section of the community to be affected
by the legislation or candidate at issue in the Citizen Panel.[49] As deLeon (1997,
111) puts it, the linchpin of PPA is that "'ordinary citizens,' randomly chosen
from a broadly defined pool of affected citizens (possibly formulated to take
sociocultural variables into account) . . . avoid the stigma of being 'captured'
by established interests and stakeholders." At the heart of PPA is showing to
the public that the laws are administered impartially, that partiality of stakeholders is curtailed. And as with Dahl (1989, 340), the considered judgment of
the pool of ordinary citizens would "'represent' the judgment of the demos."

Nevertheless, generally PPA offers little more than "carrot" inducements
and the promise of being heard by lawmakers as the primary ways of getting
participants through the door. Though their program is the one that is closest
to promulgating mandatory service, their requirement that citizens serve for
extended periods of time (usually a year) surely would test the limits (and
patience) of even the most civically committed.

Gastil too keeps his panel wholly voluntary, hoping that he can provide
inducements for service. And he is further aware of the difficulty this presents
in achieving a proper cross-section. To correct for the problems associated with
using a voluntary sample (even if controlled for demographic and attitudinal
classification), he uses a two-thirds supermajority decision-procedure as his base-
line, wholly acknowledging that his panels would be small and unrepresentative
(Gastil 2000, 228–29).[50] Instead of solving the problem directly by requiring

49. This raises an important design question: if deliberative democrats follow the doctrine of
affected interests and recruit only those members of society affected by the legislation, won't the
deliberations be largely self-interested, encouraging bargaining and other nondeliberative means
of dispute settlement? I leave this question open here; it is not relevant to settle it in this context.
For more on the doctrine, see generally Shapiro 1999a, 229. Perhaps one empirical matter might
allay a concern that people are always looking out for their best interest in deliberations: after one
of Fishkin's (1997, 220) Deliberative Polls, taxpayers "were willing to pay *at least* $1 more on their
monthly bill for renewable energy." In three separate Deliberative Polls conducted by the Texan
utilities industry, participant willingness to pay more on their bills increased after deliberations by
an average of approximately 30 percentage points (220).

50. There are many other good reasons, however, to use supermajority requirements for popular deliberative democracy. Though I won't make the full argument here (see Chapter 5 for a quick
sketch), I can at least suggest that in the context of the popular branch (a higher lawmaking

service on panels, he is content to let people decide for themselves if they care about popular sovereignty. Nevertheless, he is insistent that representation by elected officials can only be trusted when his panel system gives input into the political process. He thinks that trust in representative democracy can be restored only if ordinary citizens have some oversight and provide a civic voice to which representatives are to be held accountable (Gastil 2000, 178). He therefore attempts to design a representative panel that can be impartial, especially because he knows that referendums and initiatives do not usually draw a representative crowd. The more representative the panels are, the more likely those who take their recommendations will be perceived as being responsive to a representative constituency.

But just as referendums and general elections do not draw a representative electorate, so populist deliberative democratic institutions may be ignored and avoided by many. In fact, since they would require even more energy, they are likely to be attended even more poorly. This is why service in the popular branch must be mandatory. Nevertheless, Gastil (2000, 141–42) writes that "so long as adequate incentives are provided to potential panelists, self-selection should exclude only those citizens so preoccupied with other matters that they would be unable to make a significant contribution to deliberation if they did attend." But what about the lazy, the shy, the half of the population that won't even vote? Surely self-selection will be correlated with an inclination toward voluntarism, and it isn't clear why those with the predisposition to volunteer should be able to control policy. This should be wholly unacceptable if representation and impartiality are goals of popular deliberative institutions. If one cares to get a truly representative sample, those who tend not to want to speak for themselves will need to be conscripted for service. Since attitudinal representation is generally gauged with survey data, those who do not answer surveys cannot be represented. And their preferences are no less critical for popular sovereignty. Avoiding the voluntary response problem is simply one of the first things social scientists are taught (Moore and McCabe 1999, 265–67). It is thus rather surprising to see a refusal from most

process), there are fewer problems associated with the presumption in favor of the status quo, the argument that usually condemns supermajority decision rules. Indeed, a republican form of government, guaranteed by Article IV of the United States Constitution, may militate against too much direct democracy, and supermajorities may be one fair way to control it. For the argument against supermajorities, appealing to the problems associated with a decision-procedure that favors the status quo, see generally Dahl 1989, 140, and Gutmann 1999, 230. For the arguments in favor of the use of supermajorities, see, e.g., King 2000; 1998, Katz 1996, Levmore 2000 and 2001, Mueller 1996, 180–82, and McGinnis and Rappaport 1995.

political scientists and public policy analysts to recommend mandatory service in the design of deliberative democratic institutions.

COERCIVE DEMOCRACY?

Depending on self-selection undermines legitimacy, popular sovereignty, representativeness, and impartiality. It further vitiates the possibility for a textured civic identity and a civic voice, important probable consequences of deliberative democratic institutions. But perhaps liberalism's "leave me alone" ethos demands that citizens be allowed to ignore politics. The libertarian strain of today's vision of citizenship makes the adoption of compulsory service unlikely, and if we find ourselves agreeing with Bruce Ackerman (1991) that "coercive democracy" is eerie, it may also be undesirable. "Quite simply, we hate compulsion" (Ackerman and Alstott 1999, 204).[51]

To point out the obvious, however, our society regularly redistributes wealth, establishes federal holidays, and takes other measures aimed to ensure (read: to compel) a textured civic identity for the citizenry, and encourage a participatory ideal. Sometimes liberty and freedom demand an occasional endorsement and revivification. Of course, these efforts usually fail. Compulsory participation in deliberative bodies is one more way of trying to achieve a civic voice (though I would hesitate to be as intrusive as to require a full-year commitment from each citizen, as PPA programs tend to, or military conscription, as Kaus would).

But I should not speak too quickly because there are two senses of coercion. First, coercion results when government acts autocratically against citizens and claims for itself a legitimacy that ultimately cannot be ascribed to the considered will of the people. However, this sense is irrelevant to designing populist deliberative democratic institutions if only because they would of course be adopted through the proper channels of majoritarian democratic political life. When governments demand certain things of citizens (like jury service or taxation), as long as proper democratic procedure is followed to create the demand, coercion doesn't seem like the right complaint.

Nevertheless, perhaps there are certain spheres of life inalienable by government, so any infringement would qualify as coercion. This is the second, more

---

51. Oddly, Ackerman stakes this claim just as he argues to compel a new wealth tax. Presumably, coercion in the form of taxation is considered no coercion at all. I still (perhaps naively) think that parity in social standing can be achieved without major economic reforms, without being a "money liberal." I see the popular branch as a quintessentially "civic liberal" idea. For more on the distinction, see Kaus 1992, 17–24, 58–77.

difficult charge of coercion to parry. For example, if the majority of Americans passed a law condemning all law professors to death, we could say majoritarian democratic procedures still failed to produce any legitimacy. But tyranny of the majority is something that must extend beyond the discussion here: we have judicial review to take care of that problem. Let us keep things in perspective though: could the institution of a popular branch by an act of the people, for the people, really constitute coercion of the malignant and tyrannous sort? I cannot see it, especially if the deliberators are justly compensated for the "taking" of their time.

SUMMING UP

In general, many populist reform proposals aim to achieve more equality in "social standing" (Shklar 1991; Kaus 1992). But politics can only hope to ameliorate the problems of social inequality if the *space* of politics is renewed and extended. If realized properly, the public sphere can be a site where citizens meet and greet each other; their "enlarged mentality," where they take account of public reasons as well as their own more enlightened self-interest, is facilitated and checked by real confrontation with peers in public life. If citizens can see one another's shoes as they make political decisions, they are more likely to be able to feel what it might be like to wear them and stand in another's place. In this political space, where consideration of others is more direct, where empathy can coexist with self-interest, contestatory dialogue might help our legitimacy deficits.[52]

Political theorists and lawyers often appeal to the jury as the political institution best suited to instantiate many of the aforementioned ideals. If deliberation is a worthwhile value, the jury is a good place to start the design project. But neorepublicans and deliberative democrats alike often want the virtue of deliberation to be more pervasive in society and to be properly checked by other institutions. To this end, they promulgate various reform proposals geared toward driving the polity in the direction of deliberation. Though there is good reason to look to the jury as a model of a deliberative institution, the analogy must be more carefully investigated because, as I have explored here, there are many latent uses and disadvantages. One advantage that has particularly interested me in this chapter is that of the possibility for mandatory service, a feature of the jury that does not usually get imported into the design of

52. For an inspirational account of this kind of deliberative polity, see Beiner 1983.

deliberative institutions. I argued here that this is misguided, bolstering my inclusion of compulsory service in my popular branch.

In passing, I have referred to two other moments of overlap that recommend closer scrutiny. First, we prefer to keep jury deliberations secret. Justice Cardozo tells us why: "Freedom of debate might be stifled and independence of thought checked if jurors were made to feel that their arguments and ballots were to be freely published to the world."[53] But we now have direct evidence that controverts that seemingly sound instinct.[54] The sort of exercise I embark upon here suggests reevaluating whether juror secrecy is as pressing or as wise in the context of other deliberative forums like my popular branch, where I balance the needs of privacy and publicity. As a potential compromise, I have suggested that we allow jurors' names to remain wholly private but make transcripts of the deliberation public. The public would know what was said but not who said it. There are many ways of addressing the dilemma; the point is only to show that the jury analogy can help the designers.

Another issue to which I alluded concerns the proper decision rule for deliberative forums. In the case of the jury, unanimity is generally preferred. But there is good reason to think that in the context of self-government (as opposed to other-government), liberal democrats always relax consensus requirements, usually for majority rule. To be sure, many deliberative democrats like to make consensus the telos of deliberation. But there are a series of political dynamics that emerge when consensus is the stated goal of an interaction (Mansbridge 1983). This means that investigation into the use of the jury analogy may reveal a different, more appropriate procedure and decision rule, depending on the particular goal of the deliberative forum. Especially when the deliberative democratic institution is intended to achieve popular sovereignty in a polity that is predominantly supposed to operate as a representative democracy, a supermajority rule might be most fitting. But this is just another gesture to show how the project commenced in this chapter, exploring the uses and disadvantages of the jury analogy for the design of democratic institutions, may reveal salutary solutions for basic questions of institutional design. Most important, this method reveals why the popular branch—which also appeals to the jury analogy—incorporates the jury's feature of mandatory service.

53. *Clark v. United States*, 289 U.S. 1, 13 (1933).
54. See the authorities cited in note 40.

7

SETTING THE AGENDA IN CIVIL SOCIETY

The participatory democrats may remain unimpressed. They may feel that the popular branch limits participation in decision-making and that aggregating everyone's participation over time hardly satisfies the populist urge to have maximal participation on each and every issue area. As I argued in Chapter 5 when first countenancing this objection, I think participation in civil society might be another opportunity for citizen input into deliberative decision-making. Moreover, since another very serious criticism of the popular branch comes from those who see elites setting the agenda for the branch (and therefore predetermining outcomes), an investigation into the role of civil society in agenda-setting may assuage those concerns as well.

Habermas (1996, 307) objects that ideal conceptions of deliberative politics are "silent about the relation between decision-oriented deliberations . . . and the informal processes of opinion-formation in the public sphere." To address this objection and speak to the silence, I recruit Habermas's thoughts on civil society.[1] Precisely because the popular branch needs agenda-setters, and because

1. The invocation of the "civil society" connection is, obviously, not something new to Habermas. At least since Hegel this domain has been considered the place where the "citizen finds his social place, his standing, the approbation of his fellows, and possibly some of his self-respect" (Shklar 1991, 63). I appeal to Habermas here because his discourse-theoretic model helps demonstrate how the discourse networks that organize in civil society can gain access to political

agenda-setting usually takes place on the level of the elites, I need a mechanism where private individuals have better access to the information-gatherers and filterers who will ultimately more directly influence the agenda. Though my model achieves deliberation at the decision-making level, the question of what is up for discussion still needs to be "steered by communicative power" (Habermas 1996, 330) and must include the participation of more citizens than the deliberative assembly can accommodate. In addressing the agenda-setting dilemma, we can avoid the criticisms launched against the likes of Gutmann and Thompson that "one could quarrel with the range of opinions that [they] find 'morally respectable' and therefore worthy of serious engagement" (Berkowitz 1996, 36). Civil society, then, can function as a communicative steering mechanism that facilitates getting certain issues as well as perspectives before deliberative bodies—in this way everyone participates in the popular branch and sets its agenda.[2] Thus civil society is, on my model, "a network for communicating information and points of view . . . ; the streams of communication are, in the process, filtered and synthesized in such a way that they coalesce into bundles of topically specified public opinions" (Habermas 1996, 360). To be sure, the elite agenda-setters still control too much "communicative action" even in this paradigm, but at least they can be under popular control if the deliberative assemblies are made sensitive to the integrative demands of civil society. Moreover, because voting is no longer merely aggregative on my model, but preceded by intensive deliberation, those who set the agenda are less able to control the outcomes, the concern that makes this chapter so necessary in the first place.[3]

---

institutions and how they may remain separate as a playground for completely unconstrained talk. Civil society is a good site to practice for the agonistic battlefield of politics. Yet, although Habermas understates its role and its capacity to influence politics, he provides the basis for a more expansive use. I argue for a broader definition of civil society but keep intact Habermas's vision of discursive civil networks (though I relax the requirement that they be deliberative themselves) and his insight that civil society functions as a bridge between the "system" and the "lifeworld." Yet, in many ways, my version of civil society here is not orthodox Habermas precisely because I emphasize the need for nondeliberative processes in civil society and deemphasize any metaphysical need for reason as a legitimator. I acknowledge, of course, that orthodox Habermasians can be more extreme than Habermas himself on the legitimation reason affords (e.g., Benhabib 1992).

2. Some think that civil society can only rarely exert its influence in crisis situations (Cohen and Arato 1992, 587; Habermas 1996, 380). Even Ackerman's (1991) "moments" might be construed as civil society's mass deliberation as a result of crisis. It is instructive to note that for Habermas, however, we are always in a relevant crisis: the crisis of legitimacy deficit. Of course, as Posner notes, Habermas's crisis may be more of a German than an American concern (Posner 1999, 98–107). But just because Americans are blasé about legitimacy does not make it any less a legitimate concern.

3. It is worth noting that cycling is unlikely to be much of a concern: since citizens are voting up or down on single proposal, aggregation shouldn't lead to cycling; moreover, the

At the level of civil associations, however, I part from Habermas in requiring of them that they be public spheres themselves, insofar as public spheres are sites of deliberation. Even Habermas (1996, 308) himself seems to acknowledge the advantage of nondeliberative "unrestricted communication" as well as a "right to remain strangers" with fellow citizens. Civil society might be a layer of social relation where we are entitled to apolitical talk, ethnocentric particularism, and nondeliberative communication.

Of course, Habermas is still correct to note that civil society's pathologies need tempering through publicity in the political sphere. But civil associations—from religious groups to bowling leagues—*need not* be sites for anything more than private irrational bonding. We may *hope* with Habermas (and Putnam [2000]) that those group affiliations lead to political and collective action, but there is assuredly no *necessary* connection between the activities of civil society and the activities in the political sphere.

Yet adopting my proposal might plausibly transform how the media cover the political public sphere, which could not help but affect the relationship between the political public sphere and civil society. If the proposal in this book is adopted, it might prompt civil associations to contribute more aggressively to the political sphere. With media attention focused on citizen debate instead of sound-bite marketing, civil associations would likely respond accordingly and get involved in the conversation because they could no longer afford simply to attempt to buy votes from elites in Congress or pay marketing firms.

I follow Habermas (1996, 330) in placing a lot of currency on whether civil society "develops impulses with enough vitality to bring conflicts from the periphery into the center of the political system." But those impulses do not happen in a vacuum: institutional design can help incentivize civil society. In the best of cases, civil society can provide this link from social concern to political concern, and we can help make these connections with clever institution design. Nevertheless, Fishkin (1991, 31) cautions that "the political sphere must be protected from being determined by spillover effects from social or economic inequalities in the society." This conflation of spheres depicts our current situation of the corruption of our representative system,[4] one that regularly experiences spillover from moneyed or empowered civil associations. Yet while the sphere should not be *determined* by such inequalities, the interests of civil

---

supermajority rule in place helps ensure that at least a majority of voters actually concur with the proposal. See, e.g., Levmore (2000; 2001) for how supermajorities might help with certain features of the voting paradox.

    4. Because Fishkin's Deliberative Polls have no binding effect, his protected political sphere is protected from politics itself.

associations (often mobilized to demand a form of recognition) should have some input into the political public sphere. Without *any* spillover effects the political public sphere would project a false equality. Civil society must serve not only a "signaling" function, but also a "problematizing" and "thematizing" one (Habermas 1996, 359). Though Habermas understates the capacity of civil society to transform more than "the personnel and programming of [the] system," mostly because that is all it can currently hope to do, he is right to emphasize that the impact of civil society upon the political process is, and should be, through *indirect* influence (372). This isolation allows it to function as a kind of non-state-based social glue (Sandel 1996; Putnam 2000), while its indirection also helps cure the pathologies of homogenous civil associations exerting too much influence on the state. The first three sections of the chapter clear some theoretical ground; the final section closes how I began—imagining practical institutional design.

HONING COMMUNICATIVE POWER

To have deliberative assemblies steered by "communicative power," we could presumably try to depend upon prior deliberative assemblies to have citizens voice concerns to signal future topics to be adjudicated by a subsequent assembly. Or, we could just employ Deliberative Polling to elect candidates[5] who could be depended upon to put the "right" issues on the agenda. But these possibilities stray too far from the purpose of the popular branch. The assemblies could not be focused if they tried to address too many concerns, and the selection of candidates necessitates consideration of so many different factors and vectors that no preference ranking could really do justice to the complexity of picking a "bundle" of platforms. Though my deliberative assemblies cannot aim to constrain conversation, clearly I must have a particular (atomized) topic for each deliberative assembly of the popular branch; such conventions could not purport to decide anything if they were chaotic.[6] As I have emphasized elsewhere in the book, deliberation must be focused on doing something.

But this does not entail that the political public sphere itself cannot always be steered somehow by communicative power, or that it needs to be completely and purely deliberative. Not only is such a purist version of deliberation unrealistic; it is not even helpful as a regulative ideal. Appealing to deliberation

5. William Eskridge Jr. has led me to consider whether we might reform the Electoral College by integrating it with my popular branch. I doubt people would agree to this radical degree of disenfranchisement in the selection of the president, but it is a provocative suggestion.

6. This is a serious concern with Threlkeld's (1998, 5) idea, where civic juries decide everything.

as the only source of legitimacy is just the sort of thing Michelman (1997) argues is incoherent about discourse theory and the proposition we rejected with him in Chapter 2.[7] As long as generally elected candidates are steered by a semi-deliberative society that puts them in power, they can enjoy authority more comfortably.[8]

On an ongoing basis, however, we should expect and encourage forces exogenous to the state and the political public sphere to make claims against elected representatives and the population at large. And so much the better for the political sphere because it would open it to the competing, or contestatory, dialogue that Nancy Fraser (1997; 1995) wants us to attend to. Because Habermas's model of civil society functions as a bridge between the private lives of citizens and more public political concerns, it is a good nexus for, in his terms, the "lifeworld" to exert force upon the "system." Indeed, for Habermas, civil society functions both as a self-defense mechanism for the lifeworld to make sure it does not get completely "colonized" by the system and as a check upon the activities of the state. In my model, civil society is both a structure that helps protect the inviolability of the private sphere (though I will not develop a defense of this function of civil society here),[9] and a structure that helps exert pressure upon the framing of the political public sphere itself. With more organized access to the "system" (i.e., the state and its decision-making apparatus), the deliberative assemblies will not be suspected of being merely tools that the state can use to impose its agenda from the top down.

MILD INTEREST-GROUP PLURALISM

My use of civil society resembles an endorsement of a mild version of interest-group pluralism.[10] Civil society, often bundled into issue-specific interest groups

7. See Chapter 2 for my treatment of Michelman 1997 and this aspect of deliberative democracy more generally.

8. My argument has never suggested that we must do away with general election procedures. I imagine that if my proposal is adopted, campaigns for general elections will center around which items the candidate intends to put on the popular agenda, giving more substance to the idea of a political mandate. Indeed, that might change how the media covers the political public sphere so much that "politicization" might cease to be a bad word. I address this possibility later in this chapter.

9. This argument is omnipresent in the civil society literature; see, for example, Taylor 1989.

10. Setting interest-group pluralism as an alternative to republicanism (and its "successor-in-interest"—as Jack Balkin has called it—deliberative democracy) is emphasized by Richard Epstein (1988). I make an effort here to navigate back and forth, to have my cake and eat it too.

and other nongovernmental organizations, can have political influence that is normatively desirable. For Habermas (1996, 363), influence "is converted into political *power*—into a potential for rendering binding decisions—only when it affects the beliefs and decisions of *authorized* members of the political system and determines the behavior of voters, legislators, officials, and so forth." In my model, civil associations and interest groups could predominantly touch the authorized members of the political system by rallying potential deliberators, a primary nexus of authorized power in my proposed regime with a popular branch.

One can see how money and inequality of access could easily sneak into my model through civil society. The interest groups with the biggest advertising budgets could conceivably rally the most support; they could then gain better access to the agenda-setters and influence deliberative assemblies, albeit much less directly than they influence policy in our current regime because authorized actors are far less accessible in the popular branch. But it is important to note against such objections that giving civil associations (or interest groups) the indirect power to help set the agenda should be considered more democratic than providing them with the power to decide issues directly, which is the sort of power they often enjoy now. We currently live in the latter kind of oligarchic regime, and it would be a move of dramatic progress to try to instantiate the former. Admittedly, I want to incentivize civil society's vitality also because of its valuable social (not merely political) functions. Identity, patriotism, and other kinds of emotional connections to fellow citizens are radically important for social and political maintenance, so I do not wish to try to disband or discourage civil associations that foster such senses, even if they are forums for self-interest and not the public interest. All the better that such associations foster strong beliefs; such beliefs will make a more vital political public sphere. As William Galston (1991, 255) remarks, "Even to achieve the kind of free self-reflection that many liberals prize, it is better to begin by believing something. Rational deliberation among ways of life is far more meaningful if (and I am tempted to say *only* if) the stakes are meaningful, that is, if the deliberator has strong convictions against which competing claims can be weighed." Social standing, too, can be elevated and leveled by the actions of civil society; such standing need not rely on formal political equality within the state. When political actors rely on political equality, social parity rarely follows.

Moreover, from a practical standpoint, somebody must do the partisan work of arguing for the adoption of one policy over another, and leaving it to two political parties would limit the discussion too much. If a racist group wants to submit an opinion statement of their own for inclusion in an informational packet for a deliberative assembly about affirmative action, there is no demo-cratic reason that could justify marginalizing their efforts. In fact, such mate-rial is likely to make the deliberations and the choices that deliberators make based upon discussion of the materials more legitimate, not less so. Of course, in the unlikely event that members of the deliberative assembly ban affirmative action for the reasons provided by the KKK, the courts could easily overturn the popular branch without hesitation. Bad reasons still can get policed, but from without.

PRIVATE AND PUBLIC CONTESTATIONS

Perhaps another advantage of conceiving of civil society as I do here is that such a conception addresses the concerns of liberal feminist thinkers, for example, who "fear that the liberal version of the neutrality principle makes it possible to keep from the agenda precisely those concerns hitherto designated as 'private' according to conventional [read: phallocentric] standards" (Habermas 1996, 312). It further addresses the concerns of communitarians who fear that the Arendtian gestures in Habermas toward a plenary political publicity co-opt pri-vate life in an undesirable and infeasible manner. Essentially, both camps attack the homogenizing and totalizing potential of discourse theory (probably because both orientations are susceptible to the critique as well).[11]

Habermas meets the feminists' fear halfway and distinguishes "*procedural* constraints on public discourses from a constraint or limitation on the *range of topics* open to public discourse" (313). While he thinks that his tolerant ver-sion of procedural neutrality is unconstrained enough to admit topics from the private sphere, the private sphere itself, he argues, is left protected: "Legally granted liberties entitle one to *drop out of* communicative action" (120). Of course, others question Habermas's basis for such a distinction and see a "bias against privacy" implicit in his version of the political public sphere.[12] But

11. Since under neutrality liberalism, no textured version of the good life gets publicized, so to speak, we get a rather homogenous public sphere where issues traditionally conceived as pri-vate are not aired. And radical communitarianism suffers from a similar problem when it recom-mends staying loyal to local inherited communities that are often homogenous. Discourse theory, on the other hand, aims to find a way of coping with the ever-shifting public-private split and the fact of overlapping and conflicting loyalties. A recent application of discourse theory to the claims of culture shows this potential nicely. See Benhabib 2002.

12. See, e.g., Honneth 1995, 289–323; Moon 1995, 143–64; Strong and Sposito 1995, 263–88; Warnke 1995, 120–42; and Warren 1995, 167–200. Each of these articles, from different assump-tions and angles, lashes a similar critique. But it is Moon (1991, 202–29) who is most consumed with this tension in Habermas.

Habermas (1996, 313) is insistent: "Certainly the intimate sphere must be pro-tected from intrusive forces and the critical eyes of strangers." He knows that his version of the public sphere can trickle down into private life, so he needs a place in his schema where the lifeworld can protect itself.

Civil society provides just this protection. Civil societies are necessarily, and by definition, less juridified than the political public sphere because in the polit-ical public sphere attention is focused upon the intersubjective validity of laws. Indeed, the sphere only exists for the purpose of validation and intersubjective legitimation. By providing space for civil society in the schema, however, and by letting civil society play a more central role in politics, we can be assured that the political realm itself will be less juridified. This is desirable because with a less constrained set of access points to politics, we are more likely to be suc-cessful in attempts at experimentalism; of course, the fringes and the tradition-ally marginalized may not be any more liberal than the center, but they surely must be given some equality of opportunity to penetrate the core.

The portrait of civil society that I have sketched here highlights its functional potential as an information gatherer and filterer, and makes salient how partici-patory democrats and those worried about the agenda-setting function of the popular branch can be put at ease by thinking more carefully about the role of civil society. Civil society serves the deliberative bodies in the popular branch indirectly in thematizing issues as well as agenda-formation more generally. But it also has a self-protecting and self-defensive function in shielding the individual from invasive state mechanisms, a concern raised by the "coercive" nature of the branch. Civil society is not as repressive to individuality as state-imposed top-down agendas, even though civil associations too will often give attention to col-lective juridical concerns, congregating for the purposes of acting upon the law. Social movements that aim for legal mobilization are part of civil society too.

Because civil society floats outside the political public sphere without con-straint, it is "better suited for the 'struggle over needs' and their interpreta-tion" (Habermas 1996, 314) because no special language is required to make demands palatable to a larger public. Habermas is right that "only *after* a . . . 'struggle for recognition' can the contested interest positions be taken up by the responsible political authorities" (314, my emphasis). Thus, civil society can address the inviolability of the private with a view toward public recognition. If civil associations and social movements can get things on the agenda, and they are simultaneously a place for psychological clarification of identity, civil soci-ety is then an excellent nexus for private concerns to be voiced publicly (when collectives feel the psychological need to petition the political public sphere for recognition). And institutional design techniques can be used to incentivize collectives both to look externally and internally for validation, all at once. Deliberative politics is then properly realized as an "interplay between democratically institutionalized will-formation" in the popular branch and "informal opinion-formation" in civil society (308). In this interplay, the game of keeping the public public and the private private has the best chance for success.

THE PRACTICE OF POLITICIZING CIVIL SOCIETY

Now that I have cleared some theoretical ground for the integration of civil society into the political public sphere, I must find a practical way of actually setting the agenda for the popular branch with this marriage in mind. Is there a practical way for the popular branch to take account of all plausible positions when it convenes to deliberate upon a policy? Who is going to decide which opinions count as bona fide? Jim Fishkin? Would not interest groups with more money have more "communicative power"? And would all bona fide opinions get equal time?

Let me sketch a tentative way to address these difficult design questions.

Submitting Opinion Proposals

Anyone should be able to submit a potential opinion for inclusion in the popular assembly materials. That "opinion proposal" could take many forms: it might be an exercise in biblical exegesis; a scientific number-crunching assessment of efficiency; an argument of normative political theory; or even a personal rant. I can see no legitimate way to discount any of these sorts of arguments on content-neutral and viewpoint-neutral substantive grounds.[13] Obviously, though, we must

---

13. Again, here I differ from many discourse theorists. Because most base their ideals of deliberation upon the legitimating powers of reason, they are forced to disallow talk that appeals to versions of the good life that claim a superiority of one group over another (e.g., Ackerman 1980; Cohen 1997). As annoying as biblical arguments may be in political discussions, I cannot see how they can be left out of the political public sphere in a democracy. I suppose I may be naively hoping that these kinds of arguments just will not be very convincing. I am guessing that as public reasons, which are precisely what is required in the political public sphere, they do not tend to work. In any case, even if they work, we still have the First Amendment to contend with.

Habermas (1996, 309) gives us another good reason to allow moralists to express their opinions: "If neutrality were in addition to require that ethical questions be *bracketed out* of political discourse in general, then such discourse would forfeit its power to . . . change prepolitical attitudes, need interpretations, and value orientations." We must at least try to avoid the tyranny of reason, the effect of closing out all reasons that are not sufficiently "public" in character. Reason is, after all, just one version of the good life.

limit the proliferation somehow because we could be sure that a pamphlet of five hundred pages of opinions, containing every possible argument on a policy issue would rarely, if ever, get read in its entirety. Moreover, trying to impart too many potential arguments at a plenary session prior to breaking up into smaller groups would extend the "educative" part of the deliberations too much; deference to the best-looking expert in plenary sessions is a likely outcome of that sort of design.

But when seminar professors assign so much reading that no one can do all of it, many participants have done some of it and can make some valuable contribution, even if oftentimes participants are talking at cross-purposes. Such a scenario might obtain on the days of deliberation: each deliberator will have read different sections of the pamphlet and will have his or her own contribution to make. Indeed, each deliberator could be assigned a portion of the pamphlet and required to present the material in the smaller groups. Fishkin's research, after all, shows that people do make an effort to get informed before they show up to deliberate with their peers to avoid looking foolish (Fishkin and Luskin 1999). But now I am idealizing the seminar room a little too much; most seminars are failures anyway.

A further institutional design could help my need here for filtering and integration. When we consider *to whom* the opinion proposal is submitted, a model emerges that integrates civil society with the political public sphere in a more organized and procedurally efficient way.

More Bureaucracy

Ideally, it would be most efficient to have "Yea" and "Nay" subcommittees for each of my popular conventions (as Australia has for her referendums). In city-wide, statewide, or nationwide popular assemblies, having two subcommittees, both guided and watched over by a commission like the one sketched in Chapter 1, would be a good way to ensure that filtration is facilitated by citizens themselves—in particular, nondeliberating partisan citizens. Recreating the advantages of the two-party system for each popular proposition could help bundle the platforms into neat packages. To be sure, the leaders of these subcommittees will be appointed elites of some kind: they will most likely be influential interest-group activists that are in the public eye (and hence somewhat politically accountable), chosen by the commission to represent the side.

But the subcommittees will need to remain sensitive to others in their camp in order to rally their support, both their financial backing as well as their personnel. In this scenario, then, smaller interest groups appeal (or perhaps even pander) to the subcommittee heads—which are civil associations, not state-run units—rather than to state mechanisms directly. In this manner, more perspectives would be considered and presented.

The Recurring Problems of Campaign Financing and Voucher Reform

Of course, money is still a huge problem. Cash would still be very useful at the statute drafting stage, even if spending on advertising campaigns would require altering the medium and the message: the media blitz would have to be less sound-bite driven because campaigns would ultimately be subject to real scrutiny during the days of deliberation and may never reach the randomly selected jurors. Nonetheless, there is no easy or democratically feasible way to curb political speech to keep the rich out of funding activities in civil society. I will try to give a more satisfactory approach to this problem in turn.

Once a subject for debate is in the public sphere and docketed on the popular agenda, however, there is a way to level the playing field. The commission that oversees the popular assembly should, after establishing the question to be settled, accept applications from interest groups and nonprofit organizations wanting to be considered for public monies allocated for gathering, filtering, and disseminating information. These groups would need to demonstrate that their efforts would further the debate in some educational fashion, and that their interests are substantially related to the question at issue. Of course, each applicant would need to certify that any monies would not be squandered (but could be transferred to another qualified group); that it would not take any private monies or solicit independent expenditures after being awarded one of the coveted spots on the public money roster; and that it is not a false front for a privately funded group looking to get a piece of the public purse. Any failure to meet these criteria would result in immediate disqualification.

All groups passing the preliminary scrutiny of the commission would then compose paragraph-long mission statements to be included in a general mailing. Prior to the selection of participant-deliberators, the commission would send these mini-statements to each member of the community (the *pool* from which the "jury" is to be randomly selected), informing them of the upcoming deliberative assembly. In the mailing, each citizen would be told that the commission has allocated a prescribed amount of money to be distributed among the various interest groups included in the enclosed pamphlet. The citizen would be told that the interest groups included have agreed to take only public money, but are entitled to transfer their funds to another partisan nonprofit group on the list if they feel that their money would be better utilized under a larger umbrella. The citizen would be informed that the public monies that have been allocated for this stage of the deliberative assembly are aimed to help thematize the issues relevant for the deliberative assembly to come. The money would fund educational efforts, including buying media time, to give citizens a chance to have input into their fellows who will ultimately decide the issue at the popular assembly. The citizen would then be asked to allocate fifty points among the different groups in whatever way he or she feels appropriate.[14] Citizens would have a few weeks to complete their forms and return their preferences along with an affidavit and accompanying identification documents to ensure that the points are not awarded under coercion or on the promise of perquisites, and to ensure that each individual awards no more than fifty points. The funds available would then be distributed by the commission to the groups, proportional to the points awarded by the general public.

Many good citizens will probably toss the lengthy pamphlet into the garbage. But as long as we get a reasonable response rate,[15] this measure will help ensure that some substantial portion of the community and some new civil associations will get access to the political public sphere, actors usually reserving their activities to civil society. This allocation mechanism does not solve all of our agenda-setting problems, but it does expand who can be heard. Even the privately funded civil associations that will not qualify for public money may still want to pander to some of the smaller civil societies that get awarded substantial monies in the public mechanism. Real public money at stake for contest by the general electorate may also encourage big private money to help some of the smaller civil associations indirectly, by advertising for them with independent expenditures (though solicitation of them may be deemed illegal). This contest for cash

14. Obviously, this suggestion bears close resemblance to Ackerman's (1993) "Patriot" proposal. There are, of course, a number of differences: I do not do away with all private money (civil associations can opt out); I do not allow candidates or parties to vie for the cash; I do not prescribe in advance how much to allocate to the program or to a particular election—I will leave it to appropriations committees to figure a reasonable amount to allot, varying with the magnitude and political importance of the item on the popular agenda. But I will not belabor the differences in this context.

15. The clever will notice here that I seem remarkably cavalier about the voluntary response problem when I need to ignore it for my proposals. But I never claim that such a problem always can be avoided. Instead, I argue that will-formation, which takes place in the deliberative assemblies of the popular branch, requires true representativeness or randomness without the response problem. In opinion-formation, taking place at the level of civil society and its organization and mobilization, however, no such assurances need be made: civil society is predominantly and appropriately a site of voluntarism. Fishkin's Deliberative Polls can be vindicated, then, as their standard for voluntary response need be no more stringent than that of radio talk shows and town hall meetings, both sites of civil society and opinion-formation with no necessary (only hoped for) integrated political influence.

at the outset would inundate people with important information that would get them to start thinking about the issues even before the small sample of them is called to the proverbial roundtable.

One of the advantages of the design just described is that new subcommittees, "Yea" and "Nay," are effectively created to cater to each item on the popular agenda. To be sure, bargaining (not deliberation) would be the most likely form of communication *within* the subcommittees. But that is entirely appropriate and is just one more instance where nondeliberative mechanisms can support and help indirectly steer deliberation. These subcommittees would be heterogeneous publics (Young 1990); therefore, they would not require special representation or protection for groups because the subcommittees would absorb minority arguments to help their coalitions—and cash flows—in any case. And since the arguments of the subcommittees would ultimately be subjected to the thoughtful consideration of 525 random and representative people, they would need to make forceful arguments, not just target the right pockets with campaign contributions, as interest groups are wont to do in our current system.

Turning Back the Clock: Another Agenda-Setting Issue

I have said nothing about setting the agenda *before* an issue gets docketed for deliberative adjudication. Is there no way that the people can have better access to getting issues on the popular agenda in the first place? Of course, only people with substantial funds for signature-collection would have any hope of getting a popular initiative before the people (Broder 2000).

Presumably, I could try arguing for a public funds allocation program similar to the one described above at an earlier stage of the process, allowing interest groups access to public money continuously. But this emendation of the system would be exorbitantly more costly,[16] making it even less feasible than it already is. Moreover, with constant begging coming from so many different angles and causes, the field of public discourse would be too undisciplined to serve as the sort of jolt for focused discussion that this program aims to effect.

Perhaps there is another way to address the problem by encouraging candidates in general elections to set their agenda in line with the kinds of items they would like to see raised in future deliberative assemblies of the popular

---

16. It is difficult to predict just how much the popular branch would cost, mostly because there is no way to anticipate just how popular its mechanisms would be and how often people would want to call upon them. Nonetheless, it is obviously far more costly to provide constant public funding to any interest group that will not squander the money.

branch. Since legislatures, with the supermajority requirements delineated in Chapter 4, could send items to the popular agenda for adjudication, candidates could be assessed in terms of what they actually want to bring before the new branch. Of course, such a structural change of campaigns certainly could not be forced upon candidates.

But empirical evidence suggests that candidates would have a propensity to operate in this manner under the conditions of a direct deliberative democracy in any event. Candidates have noticed that running on the platform of letting the voters decide issues directly, can propel their campaigns: "Candidates for governor in California now regularly sponsor their own initiatives during their gubernatorial campaign" (Magleby 1995, 29, citing Pete Wilson, Jerry Brown, George Deukmejian, Diane Feinstein, and John Van de Kamp).[17] Furthermore, in 1992, the governors of Colorado and Michigan used similar tactics (29, citing Roy Romer and John Engler). With the structural transformation of the political public sphere imagined here, we could expect this kind of behavior more often. This would help voters set the popular agenda more directly, albeit through a representative body.

Also, in states that make wide use of current referendum practices, "issue activists have learned that placing an initiative on the ballot, regardless of the outcome of the election, generates widespread media attention for their issue" (28). So, one of the unintended consequences of this part of the proposal is that it counteracts the supermajority requirement that aims to dissuade potential losers from wasting energy and (public) money. Since issue salience is important in its own right, many issue activists may not care that their measures will fail to pass deliberative muster. Once they acquire media attention and heightened sensitivity to their issue, groups may, in the final analysis, resort to less deliberative (and less democratic) mechanisms to forward their agenda. And if groups just make a game out of the deliberative assemblies of the popular branch, they will cease to serve their purpose of will-formation. If instrumental rationality controls the popular branch, its contribution to curing legitimacy deficits will be undermined.

But is that really so? Will no important objective be served if they are used "merely" as a means of gaining salience? The shift of the nexus of power from the voter to the deliberator should have substantial effects on how the

---

17. I should note that Magleby does not find this phenomenon commendable. On the contrary, he thinks this sort of strategy "not only diverts legislators from the work of the legislature, but encourages legislators to duck tough issues and 'let the voters decide'" (1995, 29). Obviously, I respectfully dissent. But perhaps Magleby would be more inclined to agree with my reliance on his work if he knew how I wanted to change the initiative and referendum systems.

individual is treated by the mass media. The aggregative aspects of my proposed reform could still potentially commodify voters: interest groups could still calculate how much media money they would need to spend to get their message implanted in potential jurors' subconscious. Nonetheless, the "means of production" of the aggregation undergoes a transformation in a regime with a popular branch. The private vote, as John Stuart Mill (1993) astutely noted, is necessarily a commodity with an opportunity for exercising private interests. But public deliberation could change perceptions of interests and responsibilities and, accordingly, cure the ills Mill diagnoses with the private vote. The media, if it aims to shape public *will,* would need to undertake its own transformation to fit better with the decision-procedure. Since the aggregation of uninformed votes would no longer win policy elections, it is no longer in the media-manipulator's interest to use techniques that avoid intelligent and more detailed information. To be sure, these speculations about what might happen to the mass media are ultimately empirical questions that we can only answer by taking the gamble and structurally transforming the public sphere.

CONCLUSION, OR JUST THE BEGINNING

Since Gerald Rosenberg (1991) proved that courts are generally an ineffective mechanism for bringing about social change, political theorists have been forced to look beyond judicial activism for other hopeful routes to progress and reform. Even before the empirical realities of the failures of judicial activism were broadcast (see Rabkin 1989), the standard normative objections to activism, viewing it as undemocratic and countermajoritarian (Bickel 1962), still had force.

The model for reform that I offer here may be naïve. But the interaction of civil society and deliberative publics provides another possibility for *democratic* change. We should keep the courts and the elected representatives in place to keep the majority in check, as any good Madisonian would. But the addition of the popular branch into our institutional mechanisms might get us closer to Avishai Margalit's (1996) *civilized* society. Instead of tortuously making efforts to keep our institutions from humiliating anyone (the precondition for Margalit's decent society), we can simultaneously, through confronting each other in a face-to-face democracy, actually hope for better. And our failure to achieve even decency to this point might indicate that we should be aiming even higher (as the archer does) even if we only want to satisfy the lesser condition. When we do, if we do, and adopt a form of the proposal endorsed here, we might also have something to help the neorepublicans (like Sandel; see Sandel

1996) cure "democracy's discontent." We could point to a distinctly American procedure that could be the basis for a substantive civic voice.

But how can this reform come about? While I have emphasized throughout this book that I see the popular branch as a realist utopian vision (pardon the paradox), the picture it offers for the future of American governance is surely unfamiliar at a basic level. While I don't think it would take a revolution to bring about its existence, neither do I think the transition could be made overnight. From grassroots organizations pushing for a form of popular decision-making to political entrepreneurs taking up the cause, many preconditions could lay the groundwork for a federal or state constitutional amendment creating the popular branch.

Given our society's fetishization of written constitutions (especially the federal one), no major reform of American government could be fully institutionalized without an attendant constitutional amendment. This book has provided possible mechanics for the branch; I leave it to legislative drafters to come up with succinct language to authorize the branch, utilizing the constitutional idiom and grammar. But we have a while before that project becomes pressing; for the next few years, it is far more important to start the mobilization process that would entrench popular decision-making at lower levels of government, so that the populace would eventually feel more comfortable constitutionalizing it. The popular branch must become part of our constitutive identities before we can put it in our constitutions.

One of the surest ways to start building a consensus around the proposal is to convince political entrepreneurs to endorse a form of popular decision-making in their districts. Let me recount one example of how a politician became interested in Fishkin's Deliberative Polling: after the New Haven Deliberative Poll in March of 2002 (described in Chapter 6), the organizers of the poll provided a unique opportunity to the participants who came to deliberate. Participants were encouraged (with a small honorarium) to discuss the issues on the poll agenda with their mayors; follow-up town hall meetings were arranged wherein the randomly selected group of deliberators could share their newly informed perspectives with local politicians. Note that in this second phase of the initiative, the groups that were convening to talk with their elected officials were now discussing the issue only with members of their own towns, whereas in the first phase of deliberation the small groups were not geographically homogenous. Ultimately, the mayor of New Haven was so impressed with the deliberators that came to see him at the follow-up town hall meeting (their competence and enthusiasm in particular)—members of his constituency that he had never met before—that he called the organizers of the New Haven Poll to see if they could try to organize them regularly (once a year), offering financial support for the initiative. Another Poll, about preschool child care, was held in New Haven in June 2003, and was attended by the mayor himself.

This example shows only that local politicians still need to discover the potential that more popular input into decision-making can offer them in their quest to satisfy their constituents. Ultimately, they can help organize and mobilize their own districts to provide forums that might get the popular branch off the ground. Unfortunately, the models being offered are still voluntary; no one has been able to convince a mayor or a district to get around the voluntary response problem by requiring participation. Moreover, these models are still seen as consultation regimes, not as forums capable of making binding policy decisions. The image of the town hall is still too romantic, and blurs the potential for a better mechanism of popular sovereignty. We are still awaiting the exploitation of the full promise of an entrepreneurship that gives more voice to the people, a form of entrepreneurship that will be slow to take root largely because it relies on a large degree of delegation—and a denial of the voluntarism that makes American governance attractive to so many. Moreover, it is hard to expect politicians, who often feel they don't have enough power, to delegate it back to the people. Nevertheless, those that have the courage to do so will help get this country back on track, on the road toward greater degrees of popular sovereignty. If we will it.

Not only does the story about the New Haven Poll expose the potential for politicians to facilitate the creation of the popular branch, but it also suggests a role for grassroots activists in the process of structurally transforming the political public sphere. Very simply, without the organizational efforts taken by activists in civil society, the event never could have happened. The executive board pooled the informational and administrative resources of academics, politicians, agencies, and private industry. Moreover, coverage of the event by the *New Haven Register* made it plain to the citizens of the region that there are different forms of decision-making available to citizens; after the poll in New Haven, people could once again question the decision-procedures used to determine policy. Readers surely noted an anomaly: both before and after deliberation, participants in the New Haven Poll wanted an expansion of their local airport. Even after hearing about the environmental costs and the costs to those that live near the current, small airport, the citizens of Greater New Haven opted for expansion. So why wasn't anyone doing anything about it?

Once the traditional decision-procedures are open to question, the populace can be mobilized for more popular decision-making; it can be organized to see the popular branch as part of the American constitution, enough so that one day it may make an effort to put it into the American Constitution. Unfortunately, however, in most Deliberative Polling the priority of participation, education, access to political decision-makers, and engagement occlude the real potential of the mechanism: we shouldn't be merely polling people, but asking them to decide policy, asking them to be the decision-makers themselves.

These two components that might serve as preconditions for a constitution-alization of the popular branch, entrepreneurship and grassroots mobilization, are of a piece with what Dorf and Sabel (1998) call "democratic experimental-ism." Their vision is one that emphasizes decentralization to facilitate local decision-making through deliberative means. In the first instance of democratic experimentalism, subnational units of government bring local knowledge to bear on local problems, using various mechanisms to ensure participation and deliberation. But in the second instance, coordination and information pooling become a priority for the national government, which tries to help local com-munities and regions benefit from the novel solutions hammered out by others in similar straits.

This model, an outgrowth of the idea of the "directly-deliberative polyarchy" developed by Cohen and Sabel (1997), is instructive and attractive: participation, deliberation, and accountability are all desiderata of deliberative democrats. Dorf and Sabel (1998) go further by showing how democratic experimentalism is ulti-mately an interpretation of the U.S. Constitution. Beginning to see how this form of interaction between the local and the national can be rendered consis-tent with our constitutional principles—especially those developed to accommo-date the administrative state—is a very important step in showing those committed to the Constitution how it might recommend reform in service of popular sovereignty. But we cannot fool ourselves: to undertake the reorganiza-tion that institutionalization of popular decision-making would require, we will need to amend the Constitution.

To be sure, our Constitution may in fact support experimentalism as Dorf and Sabel (1998) use the word. It may indeed encourage the proliferation of deliberative assemblies and consultations, and recommend to mayors to utilize them in decision-making. It may recommend to social movements to press for popular input into policymaking. Just as surely, however, the Constitution does not demand binding popular decision-making. This book has argued that we should demand it from ourselves and then make our Constitution demand it from us. Popular deliberation should de-liberate us and bind us to its results.

Books and Periodicals

Abramson, Jeffrey. 1994. *We, The Jury*. Cambridge: Harvard University Press.
Ackerman, Bruce. 1980. *Social Justice in the Liberal State*. New Haven: Yale University Press.
———. 1991. *We the People: Foundations*. Cambridge: Harvard University Press, Belknap Press.
———. 1993. "Crediting the Voters: A New Beginning for Campaign Finance." *American Prospect* 13: 71ff.
———. 2000. "The New Separation of Powers." *Harvard Law Review* 113: 634ff.
Ackerman, Bruce, and Anne Alstott. 1999. *The Stakeholder Society*. New Haven: Yale University Press.
Alexander, Lisa. E. 1991. "Viciniage, Venue, and Community Cross-Section." *Hastings Constitutional Law Quarterly* 19: 261ff.
Amar, Akhil Reed. 1994. "The Central Meaning of Republican Government: Popular Sovereignty, Majority Rule, and the Denominator Problem." *University of Colorado Law Review* 65: 749ff.
———. 1997. "Reinventing Juries: Ten Suggested Reforms." In *The Constitution and Criminal Procedure*. New Haven: Yale University Press.
———. 1998. *The Bill of Rights: Creation and Reconstruction*. New Haven: Yale University Press.
Amar, Vikram D. 1995. "Jury Service as Political Participation Akin to Voting." *Cornell Law Review* 80: 239ff.
Arendt, Hannah. 1958. *The Human Condition*. New York: Doubleday/Anchor.
———. 1965. *On Revolution*. New York: Viking Press.
———. 1982. *Lectures of Kant's Political Philosophy*. Chicago: University of Chicago Press.
Aristotle. 1984. *Politics*. Translated and edited by Carnes Lord. Chicago: University of Chicago Press.
———. 1985. *Nicomachean Ethics*. Translated by Terence Irwin. Indianapolis: Hackett.

Ayres, Ian, and Jeremy Bulow. 1998. "The Donation Booth: Mandating Donor Anonymity to Disrupt the Market for Political Influence." *Stanford Law Review* 50: 837ff.

Barber, Benjamin. 1984. *Strong Democracy: Participatory Politics for a New Age.* Berkeley and Los Angeles: University of California Press.

———. 1990. *The Conquest of Politics: Liberal Philosophy in Democratic Times.* Princeton: Princeton University Press.

Baker, Lynn A. 1991. "Direct Democracy and Discrimination: A Public Choice Perspective." *Chicago-Kent Law Review* 67: 707ff.

Becker, Ted. 1981. "Teledemocracy: Bringing Power Back to the People." *Futurist* 15: 6ff.

Beiner, Ronald. 1983. *Political Judgment.* Chicago: University of Chicago Press.

Benhabib, Seyla. 1992. *Situating the Self: Gender, Community and Postmodernism in Contemporary Ethics.* Cambridge: Polity Press.

———. 2002. *The Claims of Culture: Equality and Diversity in the Global Era.* Princeton: Princeton University Press

Berkowitz, Peter. 1996. "The Debating Society." *The New Republic,* 25 November: 36ff.

Bickel, Alexander M. 1962. *The Least Dangerous Branch: The Supreme Court at the Bar of Politics.* New Haven: Yale University Press.

Bohman, James. 2001. "Cosmopolitan Republicanism: Citizenship, Freedom, and Global Political Authority." *The Monist* 84: 3ff.

Bornstein, G. 1992. "The Free-Rider Problem in Intergroup Conflicts Over Step-Level and Continuous Public Goods." *Journal of Personality and Social Psychology* 62: 597ff.

Bourdieu, Pierre. 1991. *The Political Ontology of Martin Heidegger.* Translated by Peter Collier. Stanford: Stanford University Press.

Brisman, Leslie. 1990. *The Voice of Jacob: On the Composition of Genesis.* Bloomington: Indiana University Press.

Broder, David. 2000. *Democracy Derailed: Initiative Campaigns and the Power of Money.* New York: Harcourt.

Budge, Ian. 1996. *The New Challenge of Direct Democracy.* Cambridge: Polity Press.

Burnheim, John. 1985. *Is Democracy Possible? The Alternative to Electoral Politics.* Berkeley and Los Angeles: University of California Press.

Butler, David, and Austin Ranney, eds. 1978. *Referendums: A Study in Practice and Theory.* Washington, D.C.: AEI Press.

———. 1994. "Conclusion." In *Referendums Around the World: The Growing Use of Direct Democracy,* edited by David Butler and Austin Ranney. Washington, D.C.: AEI Press.

Button, Mark, and Kevin Mattson. 1999. "Deliberative Democracy in Practice: Challenges and Prospects for Civic Deliberation." *Polity* 31: 609ff.

Clark, Sherman J. 1998. "A Populist Critique of Direct Democracy." *Harvard Law Review* 112: 434ff.

Cohen, Jean, and Andrew Arato. 1992. *Civil Society and Political Theory.* Cambridge: MIT Press.

Cohen, Joshua. 1997. "Deliberation and Democratic Legitimacy." In *Deliberative Democracy: Essays on Reason and Politics,* edited by James Bohman and William Rehg. Cambridge: MIT Press.

Cohen, Joshua, and Charles Sabel. 1997. "Directly-Democratic Polyarchy." *European Law Journal* 3: 313ff.

Constable, Marianne. 1994. *The Law of the Other: The Mixed Jury and Changing Conceptions of Citizenship, Law, and Knowledge.* Chicago: University of Chicago Press.

Cronin, Thomas E. 1989. *Direct Democracy: The Politics of Initiative, Referendum, and Recall.* Cambridge: Harvard University Press.

Crosby, Ned. 1995. "Citizen Juries: One Solution for Difficult Environment Questions." In *Fairness and Competence in Citizen Participation: Evaluating Models for Environmental Discourse,* edited by Ortwin Renn, Thomas Webber, and Peter Wiedeman. Boston: Kluwer Academic Publishers.

Crosby, Ned, Jane M. Kelly, and Paul Schaefer. 1986. "Citizen Panels: A New Approach to Citizen Participation." *Public Administration Review* 46: 170ff.

Dahl, Robert Alan. 1970. *After the Revolution: Authority in a Good Society.* New Haven: Yale University Press.

———. 1989. *Democracy and Its Critics.* New Haven: Yale University Press.

Dahl, Robert Alan, and Edward R. Tufte. 1973. *Size and Democracy.* Palo Alto: Stanford University Press.

Dawes, R., et al. 1990. "Cooperation for the Benefit of Us: Not Me, Or My Conscience." In *Beyond Self-Interest,* edited by Jane Mansbridge. Chicago: University of Chicago Press.

deLeon, Peter. 1997. *Democracy and the Policy Sciences.* Albany: SUNY Press.

de Tocqueville, Alexis. 1969. *Democracy in America.* Edited by J. P. Mayer and translated by George Lawrence. 13th ed. New York: HarperCollins.

Dewey, John. 1954. *The Public and Its Problems.* Athens: Ohio University Press.

Diamond, Shari Seidman. 1993. "What Jurors Think: Expectations and Reactions of Citizens Who Serve as Jurors." In *Verdict: Assessing the Civil Jury System,* edited by Robert E. Litan. Washington, D.C.: Brookings Institution Press.

Dorf, Michael C., and Charles F. Sabel. 1998. "A Constitution of Democratic Experimentalism." *Columbia Law Review* 98: 267ff.

Dryzek, John S. 1990. *Discursive Democracy: Politics, Policy, and Political Science.* Cambridge: Cambridge University Press.

Duverger, Maurice. 1954. *Political Parties: Their Organization and Activity in the Modern State.* Translated by Barbara North and Robert North. New York: Routledge.

Elkin, Stephen L., and Karol Edward, eds. 1999. *Citizen Competence and Democratic Institutions.* University Park: Pennsylvania State University Press.

Elster, Jon, ed. 1998. *Deliberative Democracy.* New York: Cambridge University Press.

Epstein, Leon, ed. 1967. *Political Parties in Western Democracies.* New York: Praeger.

Epstein, Richard A. 1988. "Modern Republicanism—Or the Flight from Substance." *Yale Law Journal* 97: 1633ff.

Etzioni, Amitai. 1972. "Minerva: An Electronic Town Hall." *Policy Sciences* 3: 457ff.

Eule, Julian. 1990. "Judicial Review of Direct Democracy." *Yale Law Journal* 99: 1503ff.

Farrell, Michael J. 1985. "The Judiciary and Popular Democracy: Should Courts Review Ballot Measures Prior to Elections?" *Fordham Law Review* 53: 919ff.

Ferejohn, John. 2000. "Instituting Deliberative Democracy." *Nomos: Designing Democratic Institutions* 42: 75ff.

Fishkin, James S. 1991. *Democracy and Deliberation: New Directions for Democratic Reform.* New Haven: Yale University Press.

———. 1997. *The Voice of the People: Public Opinion and Democracy.* New Haven: Yale University Press.

———. 1999a. "Reflections on Deliberative Democracy." Paper delivered to the Yale Political Theory Workshop, 5 October.

———. 1999b. "Toward Deliberative Democracy: Experimenting with an Ideal." In *Citizen Competence and Democratic Institutions,* edited by Stephen L. Elkin and Karol Edward. University Park: Pennsylvania State University Press.

Fishkin, James S., and Robert Luskin. 1999. "Bringing Deliberation to Democratic Dialogue." In *A Poll with a Human Face: The National Issues Convention Experiment in Political Communication,* edited by Max McCombs and Amy Reynolds. Mahwah, N.J.: Lawrence Erlbaum Associates.

Fraser, Nancy. 1995. "Toward a Postmodern Conception." In *Social Postmodernism: Beyond Identity Politics,* edited by Linda Nicholson and Steven Seidman. Cambridge: Cambridge University Press.

———. 1997. *Justice Interruptus: Critical Reflections on the "Postsocialist" Condition.* New York: Routledge.

Galston, William. 1991. *Liberal Purposes: Goods, Virtues, and Diversity in the Liberal State.* Cambridge: Cambridge University Press.

Gastil, John. 2000. *Back by Popular Demand: Revitalizing Representative Democracy Through Deliberative Elections.* Berkeley and Los Angeles: University of California Press.

Gordan, John, III. 1992. "Juries as Judges of the Law: The American Experience." *Law Quarterly Review* 108: 272ff.

Grafton, Anthony. 1999. *The Footnote: A Curious History.* Cambridge: Harvard University Press.

Guinier, Lani. 1995. *The Tyranny of the Majority: Fundamental Fairness in Representative Democracy.* New York: Simon and Schuster.

Guinther, John. 1988. *The Jury in America.* New York: Facts on File.

Gutmann, Amy. 1999. "Deliberative Democracy and Majority Rule." In *Deliberative Democracy and Human Rights,* edited by Harold Hongju Koh and Ronald Slye. New Haven: Yale University Press.

Gutmann, Amy, and Dennis Thompson. 1996. *Democracy and Disagreement.* Cambridge: Harvard University Press, Belknap Press.

Habermas, Jürgen. 1996. *Between Facts and Norms: Contributions to a Discourse Theory of Law and Democracy,* edited and translated by William Rehg. Cambridge: MIT Press.

Hans, Valerie. 1993. "Attitudes Toward the Civil Jury: A Crisis of Confidence?" In *Verdict: Assessing the Civil Jury System,* edited by Robert E. Litan. Washington, D.C.: Brookings Institution Press.

Hans, Valerie P., and Neil Vidmar. 1986. *Judging the Jury.* Cambridge, Mass.: Perseus Publishing.

Hastie, Reid, Steven Penrod, and Nancy Pennington. 1983. *Inside the Jury*. Cambridge: Harvard University Press.

Heidegger, Martin. 1968. *What Is Called Thinking?* Translated by J. Glenn Gray. New York: Harper and Row.

Holmes, Stephen. 1993a. "Gag Rules." In *Constitutionalism and Democracy*, edited by Jon Elster and Rune Slagstad. New York: Cambridge University Press.

———. 1993b. "Precommitment and the Paradox of Democracy." In *Constitutionalism and Democracy*, edited by Jon Elster and Rune Slagstad. New York: Cambridge University Press.

Honig, Bonnie. 1993. *Political Theory and the Displacement of Politics*. Ithaca: Cornell University Press.

Honneth, Axel. 1995. "The Other of Justice: Habermas and the Ethical Challenge of Postmodernism." In *The Cambridge Companion to Habermas*, edited by Stephen K. White. Cambridge: Cambridge University Press.

Howe, Mark De Wolfe. 1939. "Juries as Judge of Criminal Law." *Harvard Law Review* 52: 582ff.

Isenberg, Daniel J. 1986. "Group Polarization: A Critical Review and Meta-Analysis." *Journal of Personality and Social Psychology* 50: 1141ff.

Jackson, H. J. 2001. *Marginalia: Readers Writing in Books*. New Haven: Yale University Press.

James, R. 1959. "Status and Competence of Jurors." *American Journal of Sociology* 64: 563ff.

Jefferson, Thomas. 1984. *Writings*. New York: Library of America.

Johnson, Tom. 1901. "The Ideal City." *Saturday Evening Post,* 9 November.

———. 1911a. "My Fight Against a Three-Cent Fare." *Hampton's Magazine,* 11 September.

———. 1911b. *My Story*. Edited by Elizabeth J. Hauser. Kent: Kent State University Press.

Kassin, Saul, and Lawrence S. Wrightsman. 1988. *American Jury on Trial: Psychological Perspectives*. New York: Hemisphere Publishers.

Katz, Elai. 1996. "On Amending Constitutions: The Legality and Legitimacy of Constitutional Entrenchment." *Columbia Journal of Law and Social Problems* 29: 251ff.

Kaus, Mickey. 1992. *The End of Equality*. New York: Basic Books.

King, Anthony. 1997. "Running Scared." *Atlantic Monthly,* January. Available at http://www.theatlantic.com/issues/97jan/scared/scared.htm.

King, Brett W. 1998. "The Use of Supermajority Provisions in the Constitution: The Framers, The Federalist Papers and the Reinforcement of a Fundamental Principle." *Seton Hall Constitutional Law Journal* 8: 363ff.

———. 2000. "Wild Political Dreaming: Historical Context, Popular Sovereignty, and Supermajority Rules." *University of Pennsylvania Journal of Constitutional Law* 2: 609ff.

Kobach, Kris. 1994. "Switzerland." In *Referendums Around the World: The Growing Use of Direct Democracy*, edited by David Butler and Austin Ranney. Washington, D.C.: AEI Press.

Kramnick, Isaac, ed. 1987. *The Federalist*. New York: Penguin Classics.

Kruglanski, A., and T. Freund. 1983. "The Freezing and Unfreezing of Lay Inferences: Effects on Impressional Primacy, Ethnic Stereotyping, and Numerical Anchoring." *Journal of Experimental Social Psychology* 19: 448ff.

Kuhn, Thomas S. 1996. *The Structure of Scientific Revolutions*. Chicago: University of Chicago Press.

Kuran, Timur. 1995. *Private Truths, Public Lies: The Social Consequences of Preference Falsification*. Cambridge: Harvard University Press.

Kymlicka, Will. 1995. *Multicultural Citizenship*. Oxford: Clarendon Press.

Larmore, Charles. 1996. "Pluralism and Reasonable Disagreement." In *Morals of Modernity*. Cambridge: Cambridge University Press.

Larson, J. R., Jr., P. G. Foster-Fisherman, and T. M. Franz. 1996. "Diagnosing Groups: The Pooling, Management, and Impact of Shared and Unshared Case Information in Team-Based Medical Decision Making." *Journal of Personality and Social Psychology* 75: 93ff.

———. 1998. "Leadership Style and the Discussion of Shared and Unshared Information in Decision-Making Groups." *Personality and Social Psychology Bulletin* 24: 482ff.

Laslett, Peter. 1956. "The Face-to-Face Society." In *Philosophy, Politics and Society*, edited by Peter Laslett. Oxford: Blackwell.

Leib, Ethan J. 2002. "Redeeming the Welshed Guarantee: A Scheme for Achieving Justiciability." *Whittier Law Review* 24: 148ff.

Leonard, Arne R. 1996. "Emerging Issues in State Constitutional Law: In Search of the Deliberative Initiative: A Proposal for a New Method of Constitutional Change." *Temple Law Review* 69: 1203ff.

Levmore, Saul. 2000. "More Than Mere Majorities." *Utah Law Review* 2000: 759ff.

———. 2001. "Conjunction and Aggregation." *Michigan Law Review* 99: 723ff.

Lijphart, Arend. 1997. "Unequal Participation: Democracy's Unresolved Dilemma." *American Political Science Review* 91: 1ff.

Magleby, David B. 1984. *Direct Legislation: Voting on Ballot Propositions in the United States*. Baltimore: Johns Hopkins University Press.

———. 1994. "Direct Legislation in the American States." In *Referendums Around the World: The Growing Use of Direct Democracy*, edited by David Butler and Austin Ranney. Washington, D.C.: AEI Press.

———. 1995. "Governing by Initiative: Let the Voters Decide? An Assessment of the Initiative and Referendum Process." *University of Colorado Law Review* 66: 13ff.

Manin, Bernard. 1994. "On Legitimacy and Political Deliberation." In *New French Thought: Political Philosophy*, edited by Mark Lilla and translated by Elly Stein and Jane Mansbridge. Princeton: Princeton University Press.

———. 1997. *The Principles of Representative Government*. Cambridge: Cambridge University Press.

Mansbridge, Jane J. 1983. *Beyond Adversary Democracy*. Chicago: University of Chicago Press.

Margalit, Avishai. 1996. *The Decent Society*. Translated by Naomi Goldblum. Cambridge: Harvard University Press.

Mattson, Kevin. 1998. *Creating a Democratic Public: The Struggle for Urban Partici-*
patory Democracy During the Progressive Era. University Park: Pennsylvania
State University Press.

McGinnis, John O., and Michael B. Rappaport. 1995. "The Constitutionality of Legislative Supermajority Requirements: A Defense." *Yale Law Journal* 105: 483ff.

Mendelberg, Tali. Forthcoming. "The Deliberative Citizen: Theory and Evidence."
In *Research in Micropolitics,* edited by Michael Delli Carpini et al. 6: 1ff. Article
available at http://www.princeton.edu/~talim/TheDeliberativeCitizen.pdf

Michelman, Frank. 1997. "How Can the People Ever Make the Laws? A Critique of
Deliberative Democracy." In *Deliberative Democracy: Essays on Reason and Pol-*
itics, edited by James Bohman and William Rehg. Cambridge: MIT Press.

————. 1988. "Law's Republic." *Yale Law Journal* 97: 1493ff.

Michels, Robert. 1999. *Political Parties: A Sociological Study of the Oligarchical Ten-*
dencies of Modern Democracy. Translated by Eden Paul and Ceder Paul. New
York: Free Press.

Mill, John Stuart. 1993. *Considerations on Representative Government.* Edited by
Geraint Williams. New York: Charles E. Tuttle.

Miller, William Lee. 1999. *Arguing about Slavery: John Quincy Adams and the Great*
Battle in the United States Congress. New York: Vintage Books.

Montesquieu, Charles-Louis de Secondat. 1989. *The Spirit of the Laws.* Edited and
translated by Anne Cohler et al. Cambridge: Cambridge University Press.

Moon, J. Donald. 1991. "Constrained Discourse and Public Life." *Political Theory* 19:
202ff.

————. 1995. "Practical Discourse and the Communicative Ethics." In *The Cam-*
bridge Companion to Habermas, edited by Stephen K. White. Cambridge: Cambridge University Press.

Moore, David S., and George P. McCabe. 1999. *Introduction to the Practice of Statis-*
tics. 3d edition. New York: W. H. Freeman.

Moscovici, S., and M. Zavalloni. 1969. "The Group as a Polarizer of Attitudes." *Jour-*
nal of Personality and Social Psychology 12: 125ff.

Mueller, Dennis. 1996. *Constitutional Democracy.* Oxford: Oxford University Press.

Munsterman, Janet T., et al. 1991. *The Relationship of Juror Fees and Terms of*
Service to Jury System Performance. Arlington, Va.: National Center for State
Courts.

Myers, D. G., and H. Lamm. 1976. "The Group Polarization Phenomenon." *Psychol-*
ogy Bulletin 83: 602ff.

Neblo, Michael. 1999. "Deliberate Actions." Unpublished manuscript at the University Chicago. On file with author. Presented at Yale University to the Political
Science Department.

Ostrom, E. 1998. "A Behavioral Approach to the Rational Choice Theory of Collective Action." *American Political Science Review* 92: 1ff.

Pabst, William R., Jr., et al. 1976. "The Myth of the Unwilling Juror." *Judicature* 60:
164ff.

————. 1977. "The Value of Jury Duty: Serving Is Believing." *Judicature* 61: 38ff.

Pateman, Carole. 1970. *Participation and Democracy Theory.* Cambridge: Cambridge
University Press.

Pitkin, Hanna Fenichel. 1967. *The Concept of Representation*. Berkeley and Los Angeles: University of California Press.

Ponet, David L. 2004. "Multiculturalism and the Challenges of Political Representation." Ph.D. diss., Columbia University.

Posner, Richard. 1999. *The Problematics of Moral and Legal Theory*. Cambridge: Harvard University Press, Belknap Press.

Primus, Richard A. 1997. "When Democracy Is Not Self-Government: Toward a Defense of the Unanimity Rule for Criminal Juries." *Cardozo Law Review* 18: 1417ff.

Putnam, Robert D. 2000. *Bowling Alone: The Collapse and Revival of American Community*. New York: Simon and Schuster.

Rabkin, Jeremy. *Judicial Compulsions: How Public Law Distorts Public Policy*. New York: Basic Books.

Rawls, John. 1971. *A Theory of Justice*. Cambridge: Harvard University Press.

———. 1996. *Political Liberalism*. New York: Columbia University Press.

Riker, William. 1982. *Liberalism Against Populism: A Confrontation Between the Theory of Democracy and the Theory of Social Change*. New York: W. H. Freeman.

Rosenberg, Gerald N. 1991. *The Hollow Hope: Can Courts Bring About Social Change?* Chicago: University of Chicago Press.

Rosenstone, Steven J., and John Mark Hansen. 1993. *Mobilization, Participation, and Democracy in America*. New York: Macmillan.

Sabel, Charles F., and Joshua Cohen. Forthcoming. "Sovereignty and Solidarity in the EU: A Working Paper Where We Face Some Facts." In *Governing Work and Welfare in a New Economy: European and American Experiments*, edited by Jonathan Zeitlin and David Trubek. Oxford: Oxford University Press.

Sally, D. 1995. "Conversation and Cooperation in Social Dilemmas: A Meta-Analysis of Experiments from 1958 to 1992." *Rationality and Society* 7: 58ff.

Sandel, Michael. 1996. *Democracy's Discontent: America in Search of a Public Philosophy*. Cambridge: Harvard University Press, Belknap Press.

Sanders, Lynn M. 1997. "Against Deliberation." *Political Theory* 25: 347ff.

Scarry, Elaine. 1996. "The Difficulty of Imagining Other People." In *For Love of Country: Debating the Limits of Patriotism*, edited by Joshua Cohen. Boston: Beacon Press.

Schkade, David, et al. 2000. "Deliberating About Dollars: The Severity Shift." *Columbia Law Review* 100: 1139ff.

Schmidt, David. 1989. *Citizen Lawmakers: The Ballot Initiative Revolution*. Philadelphia: Temple University Press.

Schumpeter, Joseph. 1942. *Capitalism, Socialism, and Democracy*. New York: Harper and Row.

Scott, James C. 1976. *The Moral Economy of the Peasant: Rebellion and Subsistence in Southeast Asia*. New Haven: Yale University Press.

Shapiro, Ian. 1999a. *Democratic Justice*. New Haven: Yale University Press.

———. 1999b. "Enough of Deliberation: Politics Is About Interests and Power." In *Deliberative Politics: Essays on Democracy and Disagreement*, edited by Stephen Macedo. Oxford: Oxford University Press.

Shklar, Judith. 1991. *American Citizenship: The Quest for Inclusion*. Cambridge: Harvard University Press.

Shugart, Matthew Soberg, and John M. Carey. 1992. *Presidents and Assemblies: Constitutional Design and Electoral Dynamics*. Cambridge: Cambridge University Press.

Simon, Rita. 1980. *The Jury: Its Role in American Society*. Lexington, Mass.: Lexington Books.

Smith, Roger, and Dorothy Townsend. 1980. "Proposition 10: Its Defeat Hailed and Lamented." *L.A. Times*, 5 June.

Stein, Gertrude. 1994. *A Novel of Thank You*. Normal, Ill.: Dalkey Archive Press.

Stokes, Susan. 1998. "Pathologies of Deliberation." In *Deliberative Democracy*, edited by Jon Elster. New York: Cambridge University Press.

Strodtbeck, R., R. Simon, and C. Hawkins. 1957. "Social Status in Jury Deliberations." *American Sociological Review* 22: 713ff.

Strong, Tracy, and Frank Sposito. 1995. "Habermas's Significant Other." In *The Cambridge Companion to Habermas*, edited by Stephen K. White. Cambridge: Cambridge University Press.

Sunstein, Cass. 1988. "Beyond the Republican Revival." *Yale Law Journal* 97: 1539ff.

———. 2000. "Deliberative Trouble? Why Groups Go to Extremes." *Yale Law Journal* 110: 71ff.

Swift, Jonathan. 1973. "A Modest Proposal." In *The Writings of Jonathan Swift*, edited by Robert A. Greenberg and William B. Piper. New York: W.W. Norton.

Taylor, Charles. 1989. *Sources of the Self: The Making of the Modern Identity*. Cambridge: Harvard University Press.

Tetlock, P. E. 1983. "Accountability and the Perseverance of First Impressions." *Social Psychology Quarterly* 46: 285ff.

———. 1985. "Accountability: A Social Check on the Fundamental Attribution Error." *Social Psychology Quarterly* 48: 227ff.

Tetlock, P. E., and J. I. Kim. 1987. "Accountability and Judgment Processes in a Personality Prediction Task." *Journal of Personality and Social Psychology* 52: 700ff.

Thompson, Dennis. 1999. "Democratic Secrecy." *Political Science Quarterly* 114: 181ff.

Threlkeld, Simon. 1998. "A Blueprint for Democratic Law-making: Give Citizen Juries the Final Say." *Policy* 28: 5ff.

Traub, Joseph. 1996–97. "Discrimination in Plebiscites: Discursive Irrationality." *Temple Political and Civil Rights Law Review* 6: 99ff.

Unger, Roberto Mangabeira. 1996. *What Should Legal Analysis Become?* London: Verso.

Van Dyke, Jon. 1977. *Jury Selection Procedures: Our Uncertain Commitment to Representative Panels*. Cambridge, Mass.: Ballinger.

Verba, Sidney, et al. 1993. "Citizen Activity: Who Participates? What Do They Say?" *American Political Science Review* 87: 303ff.

Waldron, Jeremy. 1998. *Law and Disagreement*. Oxford: Oxford University Press.

———. 1999. *The Dignity of Legislation*. Cambridge: Cambridge University Press.

Walzer, Michael. 1983. *Spheres of Justice: A Defense of Pluralism and Equality*. New York: Basic Books.

Warnke, Georgia. 1995. "Communicative Rationality and Cultural Values." In *The Cambridge Companion to Habermas,* edited by Stephen K. White. Cambridge: Cambridge University Press.

Warren, Mark. 1995. "The Self in Discursive Democracy." In *The Cambridge Companion to Habermas,* edited by Stephen K. White. Cambridge: Cambridge University Press.

———. 1996. "Deliberative Democracy and Authority." *American Political Science Review* 90: 46ff.

West, Herbert. 1911. "Citizenship and the Evening Use of School Buildings II." *New Boston,* April.

Wolff, Robert Paul. 1970. *In Defense of Anarchism.* New York: Harper and Row.

Wright, Ronald F. 1992. "Why Not Administrative Grand Juries?" *Administrative Law Review* 44: 465ff.

Young, Iris Marion. 1990. *Justice and the Politics of Difference.* Princeton: Princeton University Press.

Cases

Apodaca v. Oregon, 406 U.S. 404 (1972)

Ballard v. United States, 329 U.S. 187 (1946)

Bowers v. Hardwick, 478 U.S. 186 (1986)

Carter v. Jury Commission, 396 U.S. 333 (1970)

Citizens Against Rent Control / Coalition for Fair Housing v. City of Berkeley, 454 U.S. 290 (1981)

Clark v. United States, 289 U.S. 1 (1933)

Duncan v. Louisiana, 391 U.S. 145 (1968)

Edmonson v. Leesville Concrete Co., 500 U.S. 614 (1991)

Glasser v. United States, 315 U.S. 60 (1942)

In re *Globe Newspaper Co.,* 920 F.2d 88 (1st Cir. 1990)

Griswold v. Connecticut, 381 U.S. 479 (1965)

Hernandez v. Texas, 347 U.S. 475 (1954)

Holland v. Illinois, 493 U.S. 474 (1990)

Hunter v. Erickson, 393 U.S. 385 (1969)

Irvin v Dowd, 366 U.S. 717 (1961)

James v. Valtierra, 402 U.S. 137 (1971)

Lochner v. New York, 198 U.S. 45 (1905)

Moore v. East Cleveland, 431 U.S. 494 (1977)

Powers v. Ohio, 499 U.S. 400 (1991)

Reitman v. Mulkey, 387 U.S. 369 (1967)

State v. Ragland, 519 A.2d 1361 (N.J. 1986)

Taylor v. Louisiana, 419 U.S. 522 (1975)

Thiel v. S. Pac. Co., 328 U.S. 217 (1946)

United States v. Raszkiewicz, 169 F.3d 459 (7th Cir. 1999)

United States v. Sparf, 156 U.S. 51 (1895)

Williams v. Florida, 399 U.S. 78 (1970)

Constitutions

California Constitution, Art. II, § 8(d)
Florida Constitution, Art. XI, § 3
Oregon Constitution, Art. IV, § 1(2) (d)
United States Constitution, Art. III, § 2, cl. 3; Art. IV, § 4; Amend. V; Amend. VI;
    Amend. XIV

Statutes

Jury Selection and Service Act of 1968
28 United States Code §§ 1821, 1861–69, 1871

INDEX

deliberative assemblies: campaign financing and, 127–29; corruptibility of, 77–78; in deliberative democracy, 17; federal statutory issues and, 72 n. 26; participatory democrats and, 79–80; as political opportunity, 81–82; publicity issues concerning, 78–79; role of secrecy in, 107 n. 40; Sunstein's critique of, 99–101; voters' participation in, 80–81

deliberative democracy: activists' role in establishing, 7; affected interests doctrine, 27; basic principle of, 1; branch interaction in, 22–23; bureaucracy in, 126–27; competing theories of, 1–2; compulsory service and, 103–13; elitist/liberal model, 31; as fourth government branch, 4; incompetence and inefficiency in, 82–83; institutional design for, 1–2, 9–29; jury as model of, 89–115; micro groups and, 26; model for, 5; popular branch as alternative to, 13; populist/democratic model, 31; representation and impartiality issues, 108–13; supermajority requirement in, 83–87; unanimity and, 43–44

deliberative democracy commission: design of, 4–5; institutionalization of, 5–6

Deliberative Polling: affected interests doctrine and, 111 n. 49; citizen competence and, 25–26; electoral politics and, 120–21, 134–35; Fishkin's concept of, 5, 10, 93–95, 110–13; limitations of, 35–40; political reform and, 135–36; protected political sphere and, 119 n. 4; voluntary response and, 128 n. 15

Democrat and Chronicle, 56

"democratic experimentalism" principle, 136

"democratic secrecy" concept, 78 n. 2

"descriptive representation," 61 n. 3

Deukmejian, George, 130

Dignity of Legislation, 31

direct democracy: deliberative agenda and, 13–14; Deliberative Polling and, 36–40; electoral politics and, 130–31; historical roots of, 59; judicial review of, 22–23, 70–73; partisan politics and, 74–76; popular branch of government as alternative to, 12–29; Progressive Era and, 53–55; structural correctives in, 62–66; supermajority requirement and, 86–87. *See also* initiatives; referendums

direct elections, popular branch members, 16

discourse theory: deliberative democracy and, 10–12, 121; of Habermas, 117 n. 1; opinion proposal concept and, 125 n. 13; private versus public contestation, 123–25

Dorf, Michael, 7, 136

double majority requirement, 73

Dryzek, John, 108

due process doctrine, 67–69

Duncan v. Louisiana, 89 n. 2

Duverger, Maurice, 50–51

Dworkin, Ronald, 18 n. 11

Edmonson v. Leesville Concrete Co., 90 n. 5

educational pamphlets: deliberative democracy and role of, 25 n. 19, 128–29; as public documents, 79

educative function of deliberative democracy, 82–83, 105–8, 126

Edward, Karol, 25, 91 n. 7

Electoral College, 65 n. 9, 120 n. 5

electoral juries proposal, 38–39

electoral politics: agenda-setting in, 129–30; deliberative democracy as opportunity for, 81–82; Deliberative Polling and, 38; direct democracy and, 105; elitism of, 60–61; failures of, 97–98; limits to selection in, 2; public sphere and, 121 n. 8

elitism: in agenda-setting, 118–31; in civic juries, 101–2; in deliberative democracy, 12, 31–32; partisan politics and, 75

Elkin, Stephen L., 25, 91 n. 7

Elster, Jon, 3, 27, 34

Emerson, Ralph Waldo, 52–53

enforceable outcomes, deliberative democracy and, 44

Engler, John, 130

Epstein, Leon, 74

Epstein, Richard A., 12, 90, 102, 121 n. 10

equal protection standards, deliberative democracy and, 17

Eskridge, William, Jr., 120 n. 5

Eule, Julian, 23 n. 17, 68 n. 16, 70–71, 86

European politics, supermajority concept in, 85–86

European Union (EU), deliberative democracy and, 33

executive branch, popular branch of government and, 14, 66–67

face-to-face interaction: civic juries and role of, 101–3; deliberative democracy and, 11; democratic reform through, 133–36; versus teledemocracy, 4
fairness, deliberative democracy and, 99 n. 18
Farrar, Cynthia, 93 n. 11
Federalist, The, 69–70
Federalist democratic theory, 31, 61
Feinstein, Diane, 130
Ferejohn, John, 105 n. 32
Fishkin, James, 5–6, 10, 11 n. 3; on citizen competence, 25–26, 82–83, 126; citizen jury concept and, 97–98; core democratic values of, 80; Deliberative Polling research, 13, 23–26, 28 n. 22, 35–40, 78, 93–95; elites in democracy and, 32, 119; institutional design proposals and, 102–3; lottery system of representation, 92; on media exploitation, 82; on popular sovereignty, 105; reform proposals of, 35; representativeness concept of, 109–10; Sunstein's analysis of, 100–101; supermajority requirement and, 86–87; on voter turnout, 19 n. 13; voucher system proposal, 22, 128 n. 15
Forbes, Steve, 16
Ford Hall Forum, 54–55
fourth branch, media as, 38
Fraser, Nancy, 121
Fung, Archon, 6 n. 1

gag rules: deliberative democracy and absence of, 27; interest-group pluralism and, 122–23
Galston, William, 122
Garrett, Geoffrey, 87 n. 12
Gastil, John, 10 n. 1, 91–92, 97–98, 102–3, 105, 109–13
Glasser v. United States, 92 n. 10
Goldberg, Arthur (Justice), 67
Gordon, John, 95
Greek civilization, direct democracy in, 59
Green, Donald, 93 n. 11
Griswold v. Connecticut, 67–68
group dynamics, deliberative democracy and, 26, 99–115
Guinier, Lani, 93
Gutmann, Amy, 9, 11 n. 2, 78 n. 2, 99 n. 16, 118

Habermas, Jürgen, 18; affected interests doctrine, 27–28; civic juries concept and, 40–45;

civil society and, 117–21; deliberative democracy and influence of, 1–2; discourse theory and, 117 n. 1; interest-group pluralism and, 122; legitimacy deficit crisis of, 104–5, 118 n. 2; moralism and, 125 n. 13; neutrality principle of, 123–25; populism and theories of, 32–36
Hamilton, Alexander, 31, 69–70, 72, 106
Hans, Valerie P., 91
Hastie, Reid, 102
Hegel, G. W. F., 117 n. 1
Hercules, 18 n. 11
Hernandez v. Texas, 92 n. 10
Hobbes, Thomas, 60
Holland v. Illinois, 92 n. 10
Holmes, Stephen, 27, 70
Howe, Frederic, 53–55
Hull House, 52
Hunter v. Erickson, 70 n. 22

impartiality, deliberative democracy and issues of, 108–13
indirect influence, of civil society, 120
individualism, in mass democracy, 32
information access, in civil society, 123–25
initiatives: agenda-setting and, 21–22; civic juries as alternative to, 4; Deliberative Polling and, 36–40; in electoral politics, 2; electoral politics and, 130; federal constitutional issues, 73; financial hurdles of, 16–17; legislative nullification of, 66 n. 11; partisan politics and, 74–76; popular branch of government as replacement for, 12–29; signature thresholds, 14 n. 9; as structural corrective, 62–66; supermajority concept and, 85–87; voter turnout, 19 n. 13
institutional design: deliberative democracy and, 1–2, 9–29; jury model of deliberative democracy and, 91–115; Mendelberg's discussion of, 102–3; popular branch and, 61 n. 3; role of voluntary response in, 110–13
institutions, government by, 12
interest-group pluralism, 7; civic jury and avoidance of, 109–13; civil society and, 121–23; deliberative democracy and, 90
Isenberg, Daniel J., 99
issue activism, direct democracy and, 130–31

James v. Valtierra, 70 n. 22
Jefferson, Thomas, 6, 47–51, 59; influence on Progressives of, 51